PRESBYTERIANISM'S
Unique Gift

CHURCH OFFICER TRAINING IN THE PRESBYTERIAN CHURCH (U.S.A.)

PRESBYTERIANISM'S UNIQUE GIFT

ORDAINED LAY ELDERS

HARRY S. HASSALL

ILLUSTRATED BY PAT MCGEACHY

PROVIDENCE HOUSE PUBLISHERS
Franklin, Tennessee

Scripture taken from the HOLY BIBLE, NEW INTERNATIONAL VERSION. Copyright © 1973, 1978, 1984 International Bible Society. Used by permission of Zondervan Bible Publishers.

Printed in the United States of America

03   02   01   00   99   1   2   3   4   5

Library of Congress Card Catalog Number: 98-68172

ISBN: 1-57736-134-2

The monograph entitled "Spiritual Gifts" has been revised and used by permission of Robert E. Shackelford, Winfield, Illinois.

Outline of chapter entitled "Thinking Like a Presbyterian" from *Meet Your Church* used by permission of Joseph M. Gettys, Clinton, South Carolina.

Permission is granted from the Office of the General Assembly, Presbyterian Church (U.S.A.) to use material from the following sources: *The Constitution of the Presbyterian Church (U.S.A.)*, Part I: *The Book of Confessions* and Part II: *Book of Order*.

PROVIDENCE HOUSE PUBLISHERS
238 Seaboard Lane • Franklin, Tennessee 37067
800-321-5692

Contents

Preface and Acknowledgments

Until my retirement at the end of 1998, my title at Highland Park Presbyterian Church, Dallas, Texas, had been Director of Presbyterian Ministries. This welcomed assignment gave me two major duties, both of which I immensely enjoyed: (1) I was to invite, welcome, and teach Inquirers and Prospects about faith in Jesus Christ and membership in the Presbyterian Church (U.S.A.), of which this congregation is an integral part; and (2) I was to seek to inform all church members as to the heritage, values, and workings of our Presbyterian system, including the annual training of all officer candidates.

I first became interested in the training of church officers when my father in the early 1940s was elected a deacon and then an elder in the Presbyterian Church and shared with me both his observations on these offices and his notes from his training. Earlier in 1942, I had begun to think theologically, as I took seriously the call of Jesus Christ in the context of a communicants class taught by my pastor to prepare me for full church membership and my first Communion. My earlier memorization of *The Child's Catechism* and the *Westminster Shorter Catechism*, together with my mother's Christian nurture of me and my systematic Bible memory work, all contributed to my early commitment to Jesus Christ as my Lord and Savior, and my desire to know God and to understand God's Word for daily life.

My call to Christian ministry came when I was eighteen and was accompanied by immediate weekly opportunities to preach, teach, and pastor, with presbytery's permission and supervision. Throughout all seven years of my college and seminary training, I had opportunities to learn the faith of the Scriptures and the Presbyterian Constitution, so that I might pass it on to others. In the forty-one years since ordination to the gospel ministry, I have served three churches long-term, plus sixteen others, some on a part-time basis, others in multiples, still others while I was a "tentmaker" renewalist; in all of these I have had the privilege of training new officers. In my current call, for sixteen years I have been responsible for the training of forty new officers per year (twenty deacons and twenty elders).

Over the years I have been a student of some of the great Presbyterians of the mid-twentieth century: C. Morton Hanna; Kenneth J. Foreman Sr.; Ernest Trice Thompson; Ben Lacy Rose; Walter L. Lingle; Joseph M. Gettys; Stuart R. Oglesby; and J. Wayte Fulton Jr.—all of whom taught me not only the facts about Presbyterianism but also illustrated in their living the Presbyterian "ethos" or tone, so essential to exhibit in our dealings with one another and the outside world. It is my ardent hope all may learn this tone by which we Presbyterians seek to follow the Living God as revealed in Jesus Christ. Such a practice would alter our behavior, brighten our public image, and prove us more faithful to the Lord of the Church.

This text was first born in my mind in embryonic form, as I was being trained by the faculty of Louisville Seminary to teach others the meaning of Presbyterian faith, doctrine and sacraments, polity, and the duties of our three Presbyterian offices. The message of this text has been used conversationally in pastoral visits and in a variety of classroom contexts. On one occasion, in a forty-member church I was serving, four new officers were elected; I was asked to take two hours on each of two Sunday nights to prepare them for ordination. The whole congregation was invited to sit in on this training; to my surprise twenty-one persons showed up and completed this four-hour course of study!

For eight years at Highland Park Church I served as the dean of our seminary intern program, where I was responsible for training an average annually of four seminarians in their fifteen-month internships. Although a number of others also taught in this program, it was my privilege both to prepare them to know what it means to be Presbyterian office bearers and to teach them how to teach others, upon their calls to pastoral ministry. A modified form of this text was used.

For thirteen years I was associated with a larger parish, which included eight congregations, ranging in size from 14 to 639 members; it was our custom annually to hold a single training course for all newly elected elders and deacons, inviting all presently serving officers to attend also. Again, a form of this text was used in my training. During that same period of time I served for ten years on the Presbytery Committee on Ministry, six years as its moderator. Often it was necessary to train or retrain church officers in various congregations over presbytery. This text served me well in those opportunities of teaching men and women the faith, heritage, core values, and workings of our Presbyterian system.

Recently I was invited to teach this course to all the elders, both active and reserve, at a five-hundred-plus member church. Due to time restraints, this course was reduced to three Sunday evenings for two and a half hours each. The average attendance was more than fifty. This event convinced me that I should respond to numerous calls from around the nation to publish my new officer training book, as a companion volume to my twin books for Presbyterian new members, *Presbyterians: People of the Middle Way*, from which portions of several chapters have been borrowed.

The four purposes of this text are: (1) to seek in PC(USA) churches of all sizes to enable those responsible for training their new elders and deacons to have a ready tool that takes such preparation seriously; (2) to assist in retooling all church officers, both active and reserve, to deepen their confessional faith, and to sharpen their understanding of and commitment to our glorious polity; (3) to offer to all churches a text which may be used in training their more mature members to be more knowledgeable Presbyterians; and (4) ultimately to provide the higher governing bodies of the PC(USA) with a larger reservoir of elders with biblical and constitutional standards based on greater personal faith and enlarged knowledge of this "unique gift" of ordained lay elders for the Church Catholic.

This book will be made available to the public at the very time I formally move to retirement from the active ministry. However, I expect to continue preaching, pastoring, developing conferences for small church leaders, serving as a church renewalist, and teaching, especially new members and new church officers. My commitment to Presbyterian Christianity ever increases.

I am grateful for my parishioners, students, and friends, who over the years have heard me introduce Jesus Christ and teach about our Presbyterian family ways. Hundreds now serve, or have served, as ministers, elders, or deacons, seeking to live the Christian life faithfully within the Presbyterian Church. These may be found in small congregations and in large. I have enjoyed sharing much of what is found in this text in private one-on-one conversations with officers-elect in my study. Sometimes I have been able to provide insights about our Presbyterian way over the telephone with questioning Presbyterians from over the nation, including disheartened ministers and angry elders. Always I seek both to be truthful (realistic) and hopeful (optimistic), in the proper balance.

I am grateful to the Highland Park Church Session and to Senior Minister B. Clayton Bell Sr. for making study leave available in which this writing could be completed. My administrative assistant and warm friend, Jean Jenney, my ally in my new officer training ministry, protected my time and encouraged me by covering other work obligations by which I was freed for this writing. I am much obliged to my colleague of many years, D. Patrick McGeachy III, Nolensville, Tennessee, for his insightful illustrations, which brighten and lighten an otherwise "heavy" approach to a delightful subject.

God's goodness is often most clearly seen in those whom He places closest to us in our journey of Christian service. Hence, I dedicate this book to my wife and best friend, Carolyn Carter Hassall, and to our children, Hal and Kelly, Kathryn and Mark, who encouraged their dad to pursue his calling at unusual hours and in diverse circumstances wherever we lived and ministered. No one could be more blessed by a supportive family and colleagues than I. I am thankful to God. May this text be used winsomely to train our Presbyterian office bearers in a greater fidelity to Jesus Christ and in more responsible leadership in particular Presbyterian churches, and to encourage all Presbyterian flocks in our obedience to our sovereign God.

Introduction: How to Use This Text

As anyone who knows me knows, I am very high on the Presbyterian Church (U.S.A.) and committed to it, yet I do see serious problems within our family. Before illness prevented my attendance at the last two meetings of the General Assembly, I had attended thirty such annual events in a row. I have long observed both the high quality and the paucity of faith and knowledge of our Presbyterian family ways, particularly among some of the lay elders. I suspect that in many quarters there are modest selection standards and less follow-up training for some of our lay elders. If such be true, then the whole Presbyterian Church and the Universal Church are the poorer for such delinquencies. Our generation of church leaders must accept the challenge of enhanced training for all our lay officers, particularly as our current polity requires total turnover of lay leadership every three years, or perhaps in some areas every six years. Thus, we have an opportunity to be more careful and faithful in fulfilling the biblical and constitutional standards for leadership selection and for enhanced, thorough training of such lay officers.

It is critical for the churches to select their officers by biblical standards, and to take more seriously the required training necessary to enable our lay leaders to serve with equal effectiveness as our ministers. With this in mind my current local church session has instructed a special New Church Officer Training Committee (NCOTC), staffed by me, to require all newly elected church officers to read carefully the church Constitution, *The Book of Confessions*, and the *Book of Order (BOO)*, to attend a minimum of twelve hours of classroom training, and to pass both an open book written examination and a two-hour oral examination, based on the requirements found in the *Book of Order*, G-14.0205.

1

Arising both out of these sessional expectations and out of my own experience training new church officers, I have developed this new church officer training text, which has been used locally for more than a dozen years, and which has been borrowed by friends in many churches, of all sizes, around the nation. This book is an attempt to take a text developed for a specific local situation, and to revise it generically to serve churches around the nation.

Through the Church of Christ Uniting (COCU) discussions of recent years, it has come to our attention that no other COCU partners (and few non-Presbyterian denominations internationally) have anything similar to our Presbyterian "ordained lay elder," an office coequal to our ordained ministers. Thus, COCU does not know what to do with laypeople who are ordained and who share equally with clergy in the governance of the church. Hence, the office of ordained lay elder is our Presbyterian unique gift to the worldwide church! This is all the more reason why we Presbyterians must select new officers with God's inspiration and must well train them to function on a par with our ministers. Out of this realization of our unique gift came the urgency and necessity for more thorough training and even more serious examinations, both written and oral, just as we expect of our Presbyterian ministers!

This text contains six chapters, each of which is designed to be taught in a two-hour required classroom session. These classes incorporate the lecture teaching method, small group sharing and discussion (led by lay elders from the NCOT Committee), and occasionally the showing of applicable videotapes. Any material in this textbook may be included in these examinations.

Very early in the nominating process all potential candidates for church office are informed by the Congregational Nominating Committee of these reading, training, and examination requirements, so that any unwilling or unable to complete these may decline nomination before their names are made public.

The day after the congregational election each officer-elect is congratulated and informed of the schedule of the twelve-hour training classes, which they must attend, or complete a make-up offered by this NCOT Committee. Each is given a new copy of the two constitutional books, *The Book of Confessions* and the *Book of Order*, and urged to begin reading and studying immediately. In our case, the new officer election is held on the last Sunday of August. The New Church Officer Training Course begins the first Sunday night in October and continues each Sunday evening thereafter through the oral examinations, which are held on the second or third Sunday in November. The ordination and installation service is held on the Sunday morning before Thanksgiving. All new terms begin on January 1 of the following year, while all expiring terms are completed on December 31.

In **Session I** the class session begins as a lay elder welcomes all participants, introduces all leaders, explains this training course in detail, and gives an overview of the following six weeks, walking the candidates through the textbook's table of contents. All are asked to complete a form (page 10), which provides data on full name, family, vocation, previous ordination (if any), and ordination/installation status. After an introduction to the Presbyterian principles of ordination and all items required to be included in the Session's examination(s), the leader explains the Presbyterian ranking of the five spiritual authorities (drawn directly from the order of the ordination questions).

The class then breaks into smaller groups for sharing of each one's personal testimony of Christian experience (pages 14–15). Included in each grouping of no more than five candidates for office should be at least two lay elders and, if available, a minister. This small group sharing should take no more than thirty minutes.

When the class reconvenes in plenary, all turn to pages 16–20 to be introduced to the "Spiritual Gifts Fingerprint," a homework assignment for the week. These completed and signed "spiritual gifts" pages are then used by the current church leadership to help place all new officers within the church's committee structure, as they use these new officers' gifts wisely. Session I concludes with a forty-five-plus-minute lecture, in which the leader teaches "Calling and Character," "Biblical Qualifications," "Suggested Standards," and "Living by Our Vows." Homework for the next week is highlighted as the class is closed with prayer.

Session II begins with a lecture on the origins and history of the Presbyterian Church, with particular emphasis on the Reformation and the middle way position of the Presbyterian Church arising out of the Reformation. Further teaching notes the importance of understanding the ethos and personality of the Presbyterian family. Reference should be made to our Presbyterian family connections. This lecture should be limited to no more than one hour, after which the plenary should move again to small groups, moderated by lay elders from the NCOT Committee. The purpose of these small groups is to begin the study of Presbyterian doctrine by discussing the "seven basic theological cornerstones," found on page 46. Then, in these groups the leaders should encourage all to write one or more theological/doctrinal questions, to be given immediately to the plenary leader. All should move back into plenary for the last thirty minutes, during which time the leader will extemporaneously attempt answers to as many of the written theological/doctrinal questions just handed to him/her. Homework for the week should be noted.

Session III may begin by the leader answering any theological/doctrinal questions held over from last week. The "Introduction to Theology 101" should be stressed. The balance of this class should review the development of our Presbyterian confessional heritage and focus on the essential tenets of the Reformed faith. By now all in the class should have finished reading *The Book of Confessions*; many may have questions for the leader and the team of lay elders from the NCOT Committee. A brief study of the questions/answers on church discipline must be included today. Homework for the week should be noted.

In **Session IV** the leader should review the textbook materials, which seek to approach Presbyterian doctrine from several different perspectives. The leader should feel free to emphasize what seems most important to him/her. Although all candidates for ordination and installation should have basic knowledge of all our Presbyterian confessions, it is imperative that all know and agree with the latest statement: *A Brief Statement of Faith* (1991). Most students find it invaluable to have the leader review the doctrinal questions and answers, found on pages 84–88; it should be noted that on some of these questions, there may be valid alternative answers which the leader may wish to provide. Constitutionally it is required that all have adequate knowledge about our two Presbyterian sacraments; this class should be designed by the local leader to accomplish that purpose to the satisfaction of the local session. The list of doctrinal questions and answers, along with the teaching on the sacraments, lend themselves to more of a group discussion than the lecture method used in the first hour of this class. Please remind one another about homework for the following week.

In **Session V** the focus changes to polity, both constitutional and local. All should observe how our Presbyterian government is meant to work and how it compares to the other two major forms of church polity. A brief review of the national map of the PC(USA) and charts of three levels of governing bodies should prove informative. The leader may wish to tell of his/her own experience in the governance of presbytery or of his/her time at a recent meeting of the General Assembly. Polity questions from the group in plenary should be addressed. Before the class is over, the ordinands should look at their local church's mission statement and discover how each new officer may fulfill its ambitions. A review of how church polity is implemented in this particular church should be included. A thorough review of all local expectations regarding final examinations should be provided, as well as instructions for preparation and completion of the sessionally approved examination process. If a written examination is used, ground rules should be noted, as well as date, time, and place of the expected return for grading.

It is recommended that **Session VI** be held in two separate locations, led by two different teams, one for the elders-elect and the other for the deacons-elect. In each there should be a study of what Scripture says about the origin and duties of that office, as well as what the *Book of Order* states to be the warrant and nature of that office, along with its listed duties. A review of how this office and this board function in this particular church should be fully explained in both group meetings. An explanation of the organization chart for this church should be given, along with all other useful functional and practical data to help the new ordinand fulfill all constitutional and local expectations. A final word of comfort about next week's oral exam and the local process for the service of ordination/installation would be in order, prior to the closing prayer.

A sample written exam is appended for assistance in preparation.

SCHEDULE FOR NEW CHURCH OFFICER TRAINING

(First) Presbyterian Church, Anywhere, U.S.A.

Date—Year
Election—Date

[Recommended]
Twelve hours of Mandated Classroom Training for New Officers:
Beginning Date—Ending Date

Open Book Written Exams
(Date Available for Pick Up and Due Date)
Oral Exams (Date)

TRAINING COURSE

Session I: Day, Date, Location, Time
Introductions/Overview of Course/Expectations
Principles of Ordination
Rank of Spiritual Authorities
Personal Christian Experience (Small Groups)
Discovery of Spiritual Gifts
Calling and Character
Biblical Qualifications—A Bible Study
Suggested Standards
Vows

Session II: Day, Date, Location, Time
Origins and History of the Presbyterian Church
The Reformation and the Middle Way—*Via Media*
Ethos and Personality of the Presbyterian Church
Presbyterian Family Connections
Introduction to Presbyterian Doctrine (with Listing of
    Doctrinal Questions)
Doctrinal Questions Answered

Session III: Day, Date, Location, Time
Introduction to Theology 101
The Head of the Church—The Great Ends of the Church
Presbyterian Confessions: An Introduction and Overview
Essential Tenets of the Reformed Faith
Presbyterian Church Discipline: Questions and Answers

Session IV: Day, Date, Location, Time
The Presbyterian Belief System
Five Points of Classic Calvinism
"The Presbyterian Church: Its Beliefs"
"The Reformed Faith . . . What Is It?"
"Thinking Like a Presbyterian"
The PC(USA) *A Brief Statement of Faith*, 1991
Presbyterian Doctrine: Questions and Answers
The Sacraments

Session V: Day, Date, Location, Time
Presbyterian Polity: *The Unique Gift*
Ecclesiology Compared
Three Basic Forms of Polity
Governing Bodies: Map and Charts
Presbyterian Polity: Questions and Answers
Presbyterian Polity Discussion: An Overview of the *Book of Order*
Local Church Mission Statement

Examination Instructions
(Written Exams Available for Pick Up Date, Time, Place)

Session VI: Day, Date, Time (Separate Meetings for Elders and Deacons) (Location for Elders: _____) (Location for Deacons: _____)
Biblical Teaching/*Book of Order* on Elders/Deacons
Duties of Session/Diaconate
Sample Organizational Structure for Session/Diaconate
Questions and Answers on Board of Deacons
Local Church Ministry: Operational Data for Elders—Deacons
Schedule/Preparation for Oral Examination

Appendix: Sample Written Examination

Written Examinations Due: Day, Date, Location, Time
   For all officers-elect (new to their office) [A Sessional Decision]

Oral Examinations: Day, Date, Location, Time
   Oral Exams, up to two hours, for all officers-elect (new to their
      office)
   [A Sessional Decision]

Called Session Meeting: Day, Date, Time, Location
   Examinations must be approved by the Session prior to
      Ordination and Installation Services

**Ordination/Installation: Day, Date, Time for Deacons, Elders, and
Trustees**

This Church's
Session's New Church Officer Training Committee

Available for One-on-one Assistance

[Personnel Listed Here]

Outline of Class Presentation

Welcome and Introduction/Overview
1. Principles of Ordination
2. Rank of Spiritual Authorities

Personal Christian Experience (Shared in Small Groups)

Lecture
1. Discovery of Spiritual Gifts
2. Calling and Character
3. Biblical Qualifications
4. Suggested Standards
5. Vows

Areas of Examination
1. Christian Experience
2. Doctrine; Sacraments
3. Polity
4. Discipline
5. Duties of the Office to Which You Were Elected

Homework for Session Two
1. Know Session I, pages 9–30.
2. Read Session II, pages 31–60.
3. Bring "Spiritual Gifts" Assignment, pages 16–20, to next class.
4. Read the first half of *The Book of Confessions*.
5. Do the Bible Study on pages 23–24.
6. Begin writing "My Testimony of My Christian Experience," pages 14–15, to be Question 1 in the final written exam.
7. Study and know Q. 9, page 104; Q. 15, page 104–105; Q. 20, page 106; and Q. 3, page 103.

A Word to the Leader
The information requested below needs to be gathered at this first class session, so that these data will be available to you as you teach and as you prepare the list of those to be ordained and the list of those to be installed. This information will also prove helpful for the completion of Certificates of Ordination or Installation of both elders and deacons and for recording in the Session Minutes.

NEW CHURCH OFFICERS
CLASS OF _____

Office to which I have been elected: _____

My full name is (please print): _____

Spouse's Name (if applicable): _____

(check one)

_____ I have never been ordained to this office before.

_____ I have already been ordained to this office.

Place of prior service: _____ Church

_____
City   State   Zip

Occupation (person's title and name of business): _____

_____

(example: Vocational Director, Plano Independent School District)

WELCOME TO OUR NEW CHURCH OFFICER TRAINING PROGRAM!

This "particular church" is a congregation of the Presbyterian Church (U.S.A.). As such, we are governed by our Constitution, which ". . . consists of *The Book of Confessions* and the *Book of Order*" (G-1.0500). Prior to your ordination and/or installation in the office to which you have been elected, you are to read the full Constitution and be examined in it to the satisfaction of the Session. Further, by action of this Session each ordinand/installee (unless exempted) is expected to complete all classroom work, studying this Constitution and the work of the Church, including the work of this particular church. This Session's New Church Officer Training Committee is here to help each one come through this preparation with flying colors; rest assured we are on your side and will help you through!

A Word to the Leader

At this point it is appropriate for a lay elder or the teacher to walk the class through the schedule by referring to the table of contents and schedule in the front of this text, as revised by local sessional decisions. Be sure all candidates for office know what is expected, the duration of the course, the time and place of class meetings, the expected reading, and all details of the sessional examinations, as well as the schedule for the Ordination/Installation Service.

This also is a good time to introduce to all candidates all members of your session's New Church Officer Training Committee.

All candidates for office, as well as all who will be involved in this training, should be provided by the church a new personal copy of *The Book of Confessions* and the *Book of Order* (latest editions), as well as a personal copy of this text. This would be the time to introduce each of these books to the class. Many such new officer training classes also find it helpful to have each one bring his/her personal study Bible.

PRINCIPLES OF ORDINATION

Please review carefully the offices of ministry (G-6.0100), the office of elder (Exodus 18:13–27 and G-6.0300), and the office of deacon (Acts 6:1–6 and G-6.0400). Also we ask that you study seriously the following biblical passages relating to church officers: 1 Timothy 3:1–13, Titus 1:5–9, and 1 Peter 5:1–4.

Review the "Form of Government" (of the *BOO*), chapter XIV on "ordination," learning what ordination is (G-14.0101), discovering that ordination's style is not of power but for service (G-14.0103). Church office in the PC(USA) is perpetual (G-14.0203); but there are constitutional ways to dissolve this relationship (G-14.0210).

Your election to office is but the first step on a long and exciting and very worthwhile journey of service to our Lord and to His Church.

> When persons have been elected to the office of elder or deacon, the session shall confer with them as to their willingness to undertake the office. The minutes of the session shall record the completion of a period of study and preparation, after which the session shall examine them as to their personal faith; knowledge of the doctrine [including sacraments], government, and discipline contained in the Constitution of the church; and the duties of the office [to which they have been elected]. If the examination is approved, the session shall appoint a day for the service of ordination and installation. . . . (G-14.0205)

Please now turn to G-14.0207 to discover the nine ordination/installation vows each will promise before God and His people on your ordination/installation day. They deal with your convictions regarding:

1. Jesus Christ;
2. Scripture;
3. The confessions of the church;
4. Fulfilling office in obedience to the above three authorities;
5. Presbyterian government and discipline;
6. Your own life example;
7. Your furtherance of the peace, unity, and purity of the church;
8. Your promise to serve the people; and
9. Faithfulness to your duty as a church officer!

Rank of Spiritual Authorities

Primary Authority is Jesus Christ, the Living Word.
Secondary Authority is the Bible, the Written Word, as revealed through the Holy Spirit.
Tertiary Authority is the "essential tenets of the Reformed Faith," as found in our Presbyterian *Book of Confessions.*
Fourth Level Authority is the combined testimony and experience of the Church, especially as determined by actions and statements of governing bodies
Lowest Level Authority is the private understanding and personal experience of the individual Christian.

We Presbyterians recognize that the primary authority in all our faith and life is Jesus Christ Himself, God's Living Word, as we discover Him in Scripture and by the informing of the Holy Spirit. The Lord Jesus Christ Himself is our chief authority, to whom our secondary authority, the Bible, God's Written Word, bears witness.

However, there are many times when we must look beyond Jesus Himself and the Holy Scriptures to discover what must be interpolated from divine revelation. When we seek this level of inquiry, we acknowledge we are heeding a tertiary level of authority and do the best we can to comprehend the mind of the Church, as contained in the historic creeds of the Church over time. Often what we seek is not available through the Lord Himself, nor Holy Scripture, nor the creeds of the Church, so we turn to the wisdom and statements of contemporary church governing bodies and believers; we sometimes find such fourth level authority among sermons, position papers, and other utterances which seem to have group wisdom of contemporary fellow believers.

The least trustworthy and most dangerous authority is self-authority; we must be ever aware of the possibility of self-deceit, either by private opinion ("I am right; the rest of the world is wrong") or by personal experience, which of all platforms of truth is the shakiest and least sturdy, for experience can be misinterpreted and embellished for personal gain and benefit. Wise Presbyterians do not trust their unique insights nor their special experiences. We test every private opinion and every personal experience by the Living Word, the Written Word, the creeds of the Church, and the perspective of the contemporary Christian faith family.

PERSONAL CHRISTIAN EXPERIENCE

(Retain the following to serve as part of your written examination!)

Questions to be answered in your description of your Christian experience:

[Note: Today in small groups, including two New Church Officer Training Committee elders and a minister (if available), each one will be asked to take five to ten minutes orally to share his/her personal Christian testimony, incorporating answers to the following questions in your statement. In addition, you are asked to write your statement of personal Christian testimony, using no more than three pages, on a form similar to the following page. This will serve as a part of your open book final written examination.]

1. When and under what circumstances did you come to know Jesus Christ as your personal Savior and Lord?
2. Name at least two persons whom God used to bring you closer to Himself. Explain.
3. List at least two Bible verses which God used to bring you to Himself. Explain.
4. Trace the sovereignty of God and the election of God in your personal story of salvation and sanctification.
5. Note any times of rebellion or struggle in your Christian journey. How has God proven faithful in these times?
6. What parts did your family of origin and current home play in your pilgrimage?
7. What part did God's church (specify) play in your faith journey? What part is this congregation now playing in your growth in Christ?
8. In what ways have you been enabled (or intend) to share your faith with some other person? Describe.

Name:_____

MY TESTIMONY OF MY CHRISTIAN EXPERIENCE:

DISCOVERING YOUR SPIRITUAL GIFTS
A FINGERPRINT OF YOUR UNIQUE SET OF GIFTS
(A Revision of a Monograph by Robert E. Schackelford)

GOAL: To Decide How You Might Use Your Spiritual Gifts in the Church

God's call comes to many to enlist full-time in work within the Church, and there are many opportunities in full-time church work, whatever your gifts or education. But remember that those who choose full-time church employment are no more the partners of God than those who are employed in the "extension department," outside the church "walls." Furthermore, those who prepare for careers outside the church "walls" still have gifts to use within the local church.

DISCOVERING YOUR SPIRITUAL GIFTS

- Every Christian has been "gifted" by God (Ephesians 4:7; 1 Corinthians 12:11).
- Everyone's gifts are needed (1 Corinthians 12:22).
- Some are more useful than others, but the best gifts are available to those who desire them (1 Corinthians 12:31, 14:1).
- Any spiritual gift may be misused, especially if its use is not motivated by love (1 Corinthians 13:1, 14:1).
- There are the novel spiritual gifts which probably are more recognizable than the more common gifts (1 Corinthians 12:9, 10:28).
- Some gifts to the early church were people who had special talents (Ephesians 4:11).
- The more common spiritual gifts probably are not as easily identified but are very useful in practical ministries. Depending on your experience, you will be able to recognize that you possess one or more of the following gifts:

1. **Wisdom** (1 Corinthians 12:8): Ability to apply knowledge.
2. **Knowledge** (1 Corinthians 12:8): Ability to gather important information.
3. **Faith** (1 Corinthians 12:9): Confidence in the goodness and dependability of God.
4. **Helps** (1 Corinthians 12:28): Abilities to assist others.

5. **Governments** (1 Corinthians 12:28; Romans 12:8): Ability to manage and organize people.
6. **Prophecy** (Romans 12:6): Ability to boldly apply God's Word to human needs (also a novel gift for foretelling coming events).
7. **Teaching** (Romans 12:7): Ability to instruct others.
8. **Exhortation** (Romans 12:8): Ability to comfort or confront others.
9. **Giving** (Romans 12:8): Ability to share time and wealth.
10. **Mercy** (Romans 12:8): Sensitivity to the needs of the unfortunate.
11. **Service** (Romans 12:7): Ministering to the needs of others.

USING YOUR SPIRITUAL GIFTS

There are numerous ministries in the contemporary local congregation which make use of spiritual gifts. The first ten of the following ministries are included on the inventory found on pages 19–20. All of these ministries are also important in overseas work.

1. **Pastoral Ministry:** Can utilize all the gifts, but especially governments, teaching, prophecy, exhortation, wisdom, knowledge.
2. **Evangelistic Ministry:** Exhortation (confronting), prophecy, and wisdom are definitely needs and others can be used also.
3. **Teaching Ministry:** Especially utilizes teaching, knowledge, wisdom, exhortation.
4. **Christian Education Ministry:** Governments, teaching, wisdom, and knowledge are indispensable.
5. **Counseling Ministry:** Exhortation, knowledge, wisdom, and teaching are all used.
6. **Preaching Ministry:** Makes use of prophecy, teaching, exhortation, wisdom, and knowledge.
7. **Children's Ministry:** Wisdom, knowledge, helps, exhortation, teaching are all helpful.
8. **Youth Ministry:** Probably all spiritual gifts could be very helpful.
9. **Visitation Ministry:** Exhortation, service, wisdom, knowledge.
10. **Caring Ministry:** Helps, service, giving, mercy, exhortation (both confrontation and comfort).
11. **Music Ministry:** Music can be a means of teaching, confronting, comforting, and giving.
12. **Communications Ministry:** Covering a wide variety of activities, this ministry, like music, can utilize many spiritual gifts via audio-visual aids, drama, filmmaking, graphic arts, radio-TV directing, and many other media.

CULTIVATING YOUR SPIRITUAL GIFTS

Cherish and cultivate your spiritual gifts because they are among your greatest assets. They are given to the Church to edify Christians by helping them become more mature, and to enable Christians to carry out the ministries of the local church (Ephesians 4:12). An orderly, effective use of spiritual gifts brings many personal benefits. Among them are these three:

1. **A healthy use of employment work.** It is possible to be so wrapped up in a job that it becomes an end in itself, an escape from problems, or even a desperate attempt to ignore God. Some people expect too much from a job, looking to it for near-total fulfillment in life. As much as possible a job should be fun, but it also should be something one can turn loose of in order to attend to other important activities. By cultivating spiritual gifts, we are delivered from abuses of employment work. What we do, in effect, is to keep the material world in sensible perspective by exercising ourselves unto godliness.

2. **A wise use of leisure.** Some people already have trouble deciding what to do with leisure time, and as automation makes even more time available, our society will have to deal with the problem of helping people with too much time on their hands. A Christian has spiritual gifts and a commission from God to use them in ministry within the church to other believers and through the church to the world. In a sense no Christian ever retires. There is always meaningful work for him to do for Christ in addition to his employment work.

3. **A clear sense of identity.** Without definite job titles, people in our society find it difficult to know who they are. God has intended that the highest and truest identity of any human being be that of "child of God." A Christian who is sure of that identity may lose his career identity and still know who he truly is. He has unique, useful gifts which enable him to express his God-given identity.

WAYS I MIGHT CONTRIBUTE TO THE MINISTRY OF MY CHURCH . . .

_____
_____
_____
_____
_____
_____

Instructions

1. Read both statements in each couplet and circle the letter of the one which best describes how you think or feel.
2. Never choose both statements, but always choose one.
3. If neither statement describes you, choose the one which is least offensive to you.
4. Work as rapidly as you can. Be accurate. Be patient!

Preface each decision with this statement:
In my church I think I have the gifts to:

1. **A.** Administer sacraments
   B. Tell the Good News to individuals
2. **C.** Teach Bible Classes
   D. Select Sunday School curriculum
3. **E.** Counsel the troubled
   F. Proclaim the Word of God
4. **G.** Assist in children's church
   H. Assist in the youth program
5. **I.** Visit neighbors in my community
   J. Financially help others
6. **A.** Coordinate church ministries
   C. Lead Bible discussions
7. **B.** Witness to others
   D. Work in Christian Education
8. **E.** Counsel those with problems
   G. Instruct children
9. **H.** Promote youth ministries
   I. Serve by visiting others
10. **F.** Announce God's judgment upon sin
    J. Minister to the suffering
11. **A.** Conduct prayer services
    D. Direct educational programs
12. **B.** Promote evangelism
    C. Improve my Bible teaching
13. **D.** Develop educational programs
    F. Preach for holy living
14. **E.** Serve by counseling others
    H. Work with teenagers
15. **F.** Lovingly preach God's grace
    I. Participate in visitation
16. **G.** Help small children
    J. Help anyone in deep need
17. **A.** Conduct worship services
    E. Help those with emotional problems
18. **B.** Support evangelistic activities
    F. Speak God's Word with clarity
19. **D.** Train teachers and church workers
    H. Teach young people

20. **E.** Minister through counseling
    I. Visit for the church
21. **A.** Manage church programs
    F. Exhort from God's Word
22. **B.** Evangelize the lost
    E. Counsel married couples
23. **C.** Lead Bible studies
    H. Help young people grow
24. **D.** Help Christian Education ministries
    G. Work with children
25. **E.** Counsel those with problems
    J. Help the underprivileged
26. **H.** Advise young people
    J. Show kindness to everyone
27. **A.** Administer congregational programs
    G. Promote children's programs
28. **B.** Bring sinners to repentance
    H. Challenge teenagers
29. **C.** Teach the Bible
    E. Be a Christian counselor
30. **D.** Promote Christian Education
    I. Assist in visitation programs
31. **F.** Preach justice for the oppressed
    G. Minister to children's needs
32. **A.** Help with weddings and funerals
    H. Guide young people
33. **B.** Participate in evangelistic outreach
    I. Visit in the hospitals and jails
34. **C.** Learn new Bible teaching methods
    J. Open my home to the homeless
35. **D.** Train Sunday School Teachers
    E. Counsel troubled families
36. **G.** Tutor disadvantaged children
    I. Visit the unchurched
37. **A.** Preach sermons
    I. Engage in systematic home visitation
38. **B.** Lead people to Christ
    G. Minister to children

39. **C.** Teach others the Bible
    F. Preach God's remedy for sin
40. **D.** Supervise the church's education
    J. Visit the ill and shut-in
41. **F.** Speak forth God's Word
    H. Work with youth
42. **A.** Pastor a church
    J. Show hospitality to others

43. **C.** Teach Bible classes
    G. Teach children
44. **B.** Develop evangelistic techniques
    J. Help people in need
45. **C.** Conduct Bible studies
    I. Do church visitation

Record in the box below how many of each alphabet letter you have circled.

	A	B	C	D	E	F	G	H	I	J	
# of Each Alphabet											
Running Totals											=45

Add up the total number of each alphabet letter circled and shade (dark coloring) your "fingerprint" profile below to indicate your unique set of SPIRITUAL GIFTS. Please turn in a copy to the class leader next week.

SPIRITUAL GIFTS "FINGERPRINT" PROFILE OF (Your Name) _____

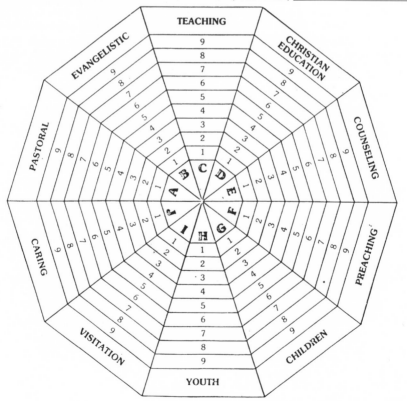

CALLING AND CHARACTER

In Presbyterian thinking there are three essential parts to a genuine "call" to the service of God as a church officer:

1. the inward testimony of a good conscience on the part of the person (acquiescence in allowing one's name to be considered);
2. the manifest approbation of God's people on the part of the Church (the election); and
3. the concurring judgment of a lawful governing body of the Church (ordination).

Both men and women shall be eligible to hold church offices. When women and men, by God's providence and gracious gifts, are called by the church to undertake particular forms of ministry, the church shall help them to interpret their call and to be sensitive to the judgments and needs of others. As persons discover the forms of ministry to which they are called, and as they are called to new forms, they and the church shall pray for the presence and guidance of the Holy Spirit upon them and upon the mission of the Church.

a. To those called to exercise special functions in the church—deacons, elders, and ministers of the Word and Sacrament—God gives suitable gifts for their various duties. In addition to possessing the necessary gifts and abilities, natural and acquired, those who undertake particular ministries should be persons of strong faith, dedicated discipleship, and love of Jesus Christ as Savior and Lord. Their manner of life should be a demonstration of the Christian gospel in the church and in the world. They must have the approval of God's people and the concurring judgment of a governing body of the church.

b. Those who are called to office in the church are to lead a life in obedience to Scripture and in conformity to the historic confessional standards of the church. Among these standards is the requirement to live either in fidelity within the covenant of marriage between a man and a woman (W-4.9001), or chastity in singleness. Persons refusing to repent of any self-acknowledged practice which the confessions call sin shall not be ordained and/or installed as deacons, elders, or ministers of the Word and Sacrament.

(G-6.0105-G.60106)

If any has a concern as to whether he/she meets all of the expected qualifications of life or witness, we encourage those to talk candidly with any of the members of the Session's New Church Officer Training Committee or with our minister(s).

STANDARDS OF "A FAITHFUL (CHURCH) MEMBER"

A faithful member accepts Christ's call to be involved responsibly in the ministry of his Church. Such involvement includes:

   a. proclaiming the good news;
   b. taking part in the common life and worship of a particular church;
   c. praying and studying Scripture and the faith of the Christian Church;
   d. supporting the work of the church through the giving of money, time, and talents;
   e. participating in the governing responsibilities of the church;
   f. demonstrating a new quality of life within and through the church;
   g. responding to God's activity in the world through service to others;
   h. living responsibly in the personal, family, vocational, political, cultural, and social relationships of life; and
   i. working in the world for peace, justice, freedom, and human fulfillment.

(G-5.0102)

Generally, the spiritual qualifications for all three offices are similar and are very high. Candidates for any and all of these offices should be sound in the faith, blameless in life, spiritual in character, and a good example of Christian conduct.

The particular emphasis laid down for the Minister of Word and Sacrament is a competency in human learning as well as a broad and approved theological training.

Elders should be full of wisdom and discretion and have an aptness to teach; "elders should be persons of faith, dedication, and good judgment" (G-6.0303).

Deacons should have a concern for those in need; "persons of spiritual character, honest repute, of exemplary lives, brotherly and sisterly love, warm sympathies, and sound judgment should be chosen for this office" (G-6.0401).

BIBLICAL QUALIFICATIONS—A BIBLE STUDY

Text   **Meaning**

1 Timothy 3:1–13

Text	Meaning
1. "a noble task"	a wonderful opportunity
2. "above reproach"	not open to censure, unimpeachable integrity
3. "husband of but one wife" (wife of one husband, inferred)	not a philanderer (does not rule out divorcees)
4. "temperate"	calm, collected in spirit, sober
5. "self-controlled"	fair, equitable, not insisting on own rights
6. "respectable"	of good community reputation
7. "hospitable"	generous to guests, open to strangers
8. "able to teach"	presents God's truth by word and deed
9. "not given to drunkenness"	not addicted to substance
10. "not violent but gentle"	not addicted to violence
11. "not quarrelsome"	not addicted to anger or censoriousness
12. "not a lover of money"	not addicted to wealth or power
13. "manage . . . own family well . . ., children obey . . ., with respect"	a good leader in own family—uses love, respect, not power
14. "not . . . a recent convert"	has observable Christian record
15. "good reputation with outsiders"	has respect of non-Christians in community
16. "not pursuing dishonest gain"	not greedy, does not cut corners, is honest
17. "deep truths of faith with a clear conscience"	has a depth of conviction and a clean heart
18. "tested"	has faced temptation/testing and has passed
19. "(spouse) worthy of respect"	family life shows Christian virtues/training
20. "great assurance of faith in Christ Jesus"	knows personal assurance of salvation

Text   **Meaning**

Titus 1:5–9

Text	Meaning
21. "blameless"	up-to-date on gaining forgiveness for sin
22. "children believe, not . . . wild"	children are Christian and not incorrigible
23. "not overbearing"	not arrogantly self-willed
24. "not quick-tempered"	not prone to anger or irascible
25. "one who loves what is good"	actively seeks to be helpful and respectful
26. "upright, holy, and disciplined"	equitable, just, devout, pious, self-disciplined
27. "holds firmly to trustworthy message, encourages, refutes"	knows God's Word, encourages good, opposes evil, and knows the difference

Text   **Meaning**

1 Peter 5:1–4

Text	Meaning
28. "not because you must, but willing"	not serving against will
29. "as God wants you to"	by divine appointment
30. "not lording it over"	not dominant, but serving
31. "being examples to the flock"	giving others a model of what Christ can do in one's life
32. "you will receive crown of glory"	accountable to God; rewarded by God

SUGGESTED STANDARDS FOR PRESBYTERIAN ORDINANDS

Presbyterian ordinands should recognize that in the Bible we have the revealed Word of God written. The Bible, our only infallible rule of faith and practice, is inspired by God in a way distinctive and superior to the inspiration of the classics or modern sermons. God spoke through holy leaders of old to record His will for humankind concerning what people are to believe about God and what duty God requires of us. Presbyterian ordinands have a duty to proclaim with conviction the inspiration of the Bible, the superiority of the Bible, and the absolute authority of the Bible over the lives of God's people. Human beings may yield allegiance to many different authorities, but Presbyterian ordinands have only one ultimate authority, the Bible.

Presbyterian ordinands should believe that "God is a Spirit, infinite, eternal, and unchangeable, in His being, wisdom, power, holiness, justice, goodness, and truth." They should rejoice to remind their associates that God has revealed Himself as Trinity: God the Father, God the Son, and God the Holy Spirit. They should teach that God the Father is the Creator of all things, as well as the Sustainer and Provider of Life. They should acknowledge that Jesus Christ is the only begotten Son of God and is very God of very God as well as very man of very man. They should believe that God the Holy Spirit is a Person, actively accomplishing the work of God today in this world in the hearts of God's people.

Presbyterian ordinands should never leave any doubt that they recognize Jesus Christ to be the God-man sent to save the world from sin. Jesus Christ, born of a virgin, is the Word made flesh. He is absolutely divine. His purpose in being born in a state of humiliation was to give His life as a ransom for many. He came to die in the place of sinners.

The biblical doctrine of the substitutionary atonement must be believed by Presbyterian ordinands. They must recognize that Christianity is a religion of blood, the blood of Jesus Christ by which the sins of believers are washed away. The preaching of the Cross as the only way of salvation is foolishness to the world, but it is the power of God to sincere ordinands. The sins of every one deserve the full wrath and curse of God, but forgiveness of sins is found only in genuine commitment to Jesus Christ as Savior and Lord and a spiritual regeneration or new birth. No one should ever have to question whether Presbyterian ordinands are born-again Christians, people who have personally had applied the blood of Christ to their own sins.

Presbyterian ordinands honor the whole Bible. They recognize the validity of the Old Testament as well as the New Testament. Since they worship the God of Creation, the only Omnipotent, they have no hesitation in accepting the miracle accounts of the Old and New Testaments at face value. The miracles performed by Jesus are not explained away; they are not stumbling blocks to faith, but road signs pointing to the power of the Savior.

Presbyterian ordinands must agree wholeheartedly with the doctrine of the physical resurrection of Jesus Christ, as He overcame the grave, death, and sin, and all the powers of Satan. Because He arose, believers too are assured of their resurrection to be with Him forever. The doctrine of the resurrection is the keystone of Christian and Presbyterian theology.

Presbyterian ordinands have taken a vow to "receive and adopt the essential tenets of the Reformed faith as expressed in the confessions of the church as authentic and reliable expositions of what Scripture leads us to believe and do." Further, they have promised to be "instructed and led by those confessions as (they) lead the people of God . . . continually guided by these confessions." Thus, Presbyterian ordinands should never be found guilty of denying or abusing these documents. They must uphold them and the particular interpretation contained therein, to the degree that they properly reflect the plain teachings of Scripture. They should recognize that these confessions, and all efforts of human beings, are ultimately to be judged by Scripture.

Presbyterian ordinands must understand that all are condemned by their own sins. The condemnation due to sins is eternal darkness or hell. However, the gospel of grace declares that sinners who repent of sin and truly turn from them to Jesus Christ in faith are forgiven and cleansed of all unrighteousness. They are adopted as children of God and are rewarded with the free gift of grace—eternal life—which includes a new destiny for all eternity, heaven. The reality of these concepts must not be questioned by Presbyterian ordinands.

The total depravity of humanity is recognized as true, despite the false brightness of modern humanism. The call of God to those who believe is sure, and God's elect can never be plucked from His hand.

The assurance of salvation, then, is possible where the Spirit works. These facts are affirmed by true Presbyterian ordinands.

Presbyterian ordinands must acknowledge that the punishment for the sinner who does not believe in Jesus Christ is judgment at the last day before the judgment seat of Christ, at which time these ungodly receive their just rewards of eternal damnation. This judgment takes place at the second coming of Jesus Christ when He shall return bodily to reclaim His Own and to consummate the age of time and history which He began. His return, indeed, is imminent.

Presbyterian ordinands must demonstrate a confident trust in the work of the Holy Spirit within the Christian Church. They must recognize the Church as an instrument of God in this age, an imperfect instrument to be sure, but one blessed by God. The Church is found wherever God's people meet to hear His Word properly preached, to celebrate His sacraments properly, and His discipline is graciously and redemptively applied. But, the Church always stands under the judgment of the ultimate authority, the Holy Scripture, and therefore is ever in need of reformation by the Word, as the Spirit interprets.

Presbyterian ordinands must teach and live an example of the Christian life of purity. The saints—God's called-out people—should live as saints of God everywhere. Their lives should be distinctive and different. Their values and goals in life must be peculiarly above those of the world. Ultimately, the test of purity of life is the true test of one's beliefs. The orthodox Christian is the Christian with the clean life, one following in the steps of the Master.

Presbyterian ordinands, convinced of their own call from God and committed to God's Word, seek to move out into the world in mission both to "the lost" and to "the poor" in twin ministries of evangelism and justice, both as a part of their church life and as a part of their witness in the world of work/school/recreation. Stewardship of all of one's resources—time, talent, treasure—is an obvious result of one's call into these offices of service.

LIVING BY OUR VOWS

Presbyterian Christians are accepted into church membership when they take explicit vows of fealty to Christ and His Church. By definition a "vow" is a "solemn promise made as unto the Lord."

A Word to the Leader
The following Church Membership Vows originated in the PCUS and are enthusiastically used in my local church. If your session uses a different set of questions, please, at this time, remind your officers-elect of them and their meaning.

Thus, all members of this particular church have solemnly entered into these specific vows of church membership:

1. Do you acknowledge yourselves to be sinners in the sight of God, justly deserving God's displeasure, and without hope except in God's sovereign mercy?
2. Do you believe in the Lord Jesus Christ as the Son of God and Savior of sinners, and do you receive and depend upon Christ alone for your salvation as offered in the gospel?
3. Do you now resolve and promise, in humble reliance upon the grace of the Holy Spirit, that you will endeavor to live as becomes the followers of Christ?
4. Do you promise to serve Christ in the Church by supporting and participating in its service to God and its ministry to others to the best of your ability?
5. Do you submit yourselves to the government and discipline of the Church and promise to further its purity and peace?

Furthermore, every officer of this particular church also has entered into further vows of vocational fidelity to Christ and His Church, whether they are our ministers, our elders, or our deacons, through the following vows made in the presence of the congregation and as unto the Lord:

1. Do you trust in Jesus Christ your Savior, acknowledge him Lord of all and Head of the Church, and through him believe in one God, Father, Son, and Holy Spirit?

2. Do you accept the Scriptures of the Old and New Testaments to be, by the Holy Spirit, the unique and authoritative witness to Jesus Christ in the Church universal, and God's Word to you?

3. Do you sincerely receive and adopt the essential tenets of the Reformed faith as expressed in the confessions of our church as authentic and reliable expositions of what Scripture leads us to believe and do, and will you be instructed and led by those confessions as you lead the people of God?

4. a. (For minister) Will you be a minister of the Word and Sacrament in obedience to Jesus Christ, under the authority of Scripture, and continually guided by our confessions?

   b. (For elder/deacon) Will you fulfill your office in obedience to Jesus Christ, under the authority of Scripture, and be continually guided by our confessions?

5. Will you be governed by our church's polity, and will you abide by its discipline? Will you be a friend among your colleagues in ministry, working with them, subject to the ordering of God's Word and Spirit?

6. Will you in your own life seek to follow the Lord Jesus Christ, love your neighbors, and work for the reconciliation of the world?

7. Do you promise to further the peace, unity, and purity of the Church?

8. Will you seek to serve the people with energy, intelligence, imagination, and love?

9. a. (For minister) Will you be a faithful minister, proclaiming the good news in Word and Sacrament, teaching faith, and caring for people? Will you be active in government and discipline, serving in the governing bodies of the church; and in your ministry, will you try to show the love and justice of Jesus Christ?

   b. (For elder) Will you be a faithful elder, watching over the people, providing for their worship, nurture, and service? Will you share in government and discipline, serving in governing bodies of the Church, and in your ministry will you try to show the love and justice of Jesus Christ?

   c. (For deacon) Will you be a faithful deacon, teaching charity, urging concern, and directing the people's help to the friendless and those in need? In your ministry will you try to show the love and justice of Jesus Christ?

G-14.0207; G-14.0405(b)

In electing and ordaining and/or installing every minister, elder, and deacon the congregation takes further vows committing themselves to "accept, encourage, respect, and follow" their church officers, as they "guide us, serving Jesus Christ, who alone is Head of the Church," as follows:

1. a. (For minister) Do we, the members of the church, accept
    (name)_____as our pastor (associate
    pastor), chosen by God through the voice of this congregation to
    guide us in the way of Jesus Christ?
    b. (For elder/deacon) Do we, the members of the church, accept
    (names)_____as elders or deacons, chosen
    by God through the voice of this congregation to lead us in the way
    of Jesus Christ?
2. a. (For minister) Do we agree to encourage him (her), to respect his
    (her) decisions, and to follow as he (she) guides us, serving Jesus
    Christ, who alone is Head of the Church?
    b. (For elder/deacon) Do we agree to encourage them, to respect
    their decisions, and to follow as they guide us, serving Jesus Christ,
    who alone is Head of the Church?
3. (For minister) Do we promise to pay him (her) fairly and provide for
    his (her) welfare as he (she) works among us; to stand by him (her)
    in trouble and share his (her) joys? Will we listen to the word he (she)
    preaches, welcome his (her) pastoral care, and honor his (her)
    authority as he (she) seeks to honor and obey Jesus Christ our Lord?
    G-14.0208; G-14.0510

No one of us should ever forget these vows we have taken before
the Lord respecting our personal relationships to Christ, His Church,
and His church officers (ministers/elders/deacons). Fulfillment of
these vows should reduce conflict in the body ecclesiastic without
muzzling genuine differences among Christian brothers and sisters.

We must remember that all these vows were taken before God in
a church constitutionally a part of the Presbyterian Church (U.S.A.).
We must be aware that each set of vows explicitly committed us to a
certain respect and support of the Presbyterian Church (U.S.A.) and
its "peace, unity, and purity." If we differ, we must differ as in family
and among persons who are nevertheless held together by a common
love and a common set of commitments.

Note that in the PC(USA) *Book of Order* "Church" is capitalized when it refers to the denomination and/or to the Church universal. "Church" is not capitalized when it refers to a
particular church, such as our congregation.

OUTLINE OF CLASS PRESENTATION

Lecture
1. Origins and History of the Presbyterian Church
2. The Reformation and the Middle Way—*Via Media*
3. Ethos and Personality of the Presbyterian Church

Small Groups Discussion and Response
1. Introduction to Presbyterian Doctrine
2. Listing of Doctrinal Questions
3. Doctrinal Questions Answered

***Via Media* Presbyterianism**
1. A Biblical/Evangelical People
2. A Reasonable/Moderate People
3. An Ecumenical/Inclusive People
4. A Compassionate/Caring People
5. A Negotiating/Process People
6. A Studying/Thinking People
7. An Orthodox/Confessional People

Homework for Session Three
1. Know Session II, pages 31–60.
2. Read Session III, pages 61–72.
3. Finish reading *The Book of Confessions*.
4. Study Exodus 18:13–27 and Acts 6:1–7 (for origins of offices of Elder and Deacon).
5. Know seven couplets descriptive of *Via Media* Presbyterianism.
6. Be able to describe how *Via Media* Presbyterianism works out in at least seven practical ways. (See pages 40–41, 47–49.)
7. Understand what is the chief weakness of Presbyterianism and why (pages 51–52).
8. Know and be able to explain "the threefold Protestant Reformation."

ORIGINS AND HISTORY OF THE PRESBYTERIAN CHURCH

A Word to the Leader

The leader may wish to use this section (pages 32–39) as background reading and refer only to those parts appropriate for answering the questions raised by his/her class. We recommend emphasis in today's lecture on the material found in pages 40–58.

The history of the Presbyterian Church is the same as the history of Western Christianity until the appearance of John Calvin in the early 1500s. This is not to say that there are not some traces of the particular perspective which came to be embraced by John Calvin and his followers as far back as the early Old Testament days. It is to say that there is no separate history for Presbyterianism until the Protestant Reformation. Thus, we Presbyterians, for better or worse, must claim the history of Western Christianity and particularly that of the Roman Catholic Church as ours, until John Calvin came on the scene.

Certainly, within Scripture itself, we Presbyterians could claim Abraham's faith in obeying a call from God to go in a land unknown; Joseph's confidence in the sovereignty and goodness of God; Jethro's wisdom in urging his son-in-law Moses to name elders to assist him in governance; Isaiah's understanding of the exceedingly heinousness of sin and the holiness of God; Jesus' teaching regarding the Father's ability to pass Him the cup of the Cross for the salvation of believing humankind; Paul's theological system of God's grace and election and sovereignty; and John's proclamation of God's ultimate victory over death, as all these are keystone building blocks of the Presbyterian belief-system.

Following the era of Jesus and the apostles, the early church struggled in a hostile world to find breathing space, persecuted by a hostile Jewish parent and a jealous Roman empire. These early Christians, many living in the catacombs, often paid for this faith with their lives. They fought the heresies of Gnosticism and Antinomianism, the Judaizers, the Marcionites, and the Montanites. "The blood of the martyrs became the seed of the Church," as it expanded gradually as an outlaw faith throughout the Greco-Roman world, to Africa and to parts of Asia and India.

ca. A.D. 30—Jesus was crucified; Peter preached at Pentecost

ca. 35—Stephen was martyred; Saul of Tarsus was converted

ca. 46—The first General Assembly (Council of Jerusalem) was held

ca. 96—The writing of the New Testament was completed

150—Justin Martyr authored his *First Apology*

230—Church structures were publicly built

303—Diocletian began his great persecution

When Emperor Constantine in A.D. 312 became a Christian, the faith for both better and worse became legal and expanded like a wildfire, though not always were the new adherents "profitable servants." The church soon became seduced with power, and for three hundred years in the time of the "Christian Empire" true believers faced great difficulties in keeping to the simple biblical faith when many sought to use the trappings of Christianity for their own glory. Augustine's *City of God* taught many concepts later adopted and supported by Presbyterians.

A.D. 312—Emperor Constantine was converted

325—First Council of Nicea was convened

381—Rome made Christianity the state religion

386—Augustine accepted Jesus Christ as Savior and Lord

405—Jerome completed the Latin Bible, the *Vulgate*

410—The Visigoths sacked Rome

440—Leo the Great was made Bishop of Rome

451—The Council of Chalcedon was convened

540—Benedict created his monastic *Rule*

When Gregory was elected Pope of Rome, the Christian Middle Ages began. Conflict was inevitable between the Christianized pagans/the paganized Christians of Rome and the barbarians of both North Africa and Central and Eastern Europe who swept into Rome itself on numerous occasions destroying all in their path. The Roman Empire eventually became the Holy Roman Empire as church and state in Rome became identical. As masses were baptized, their paganism overwhelmed biblical faith. The Holy Roman Empire sent thousands of monks as missionaries to the pagan peoples of Europe; gradually tribe after tribe accepted some kind of faith in this "Christ" and submitted to Roman authority. In these Middle Ages, called Medieval, "Christendom," with its mixtures of good and bad, Christ and Rome, church and state, paganism and faith, became a reality.

Conflict became inevitable again between the weakened West (Rome) and the challenging East (Constantinople). By A.D. 1054 the East and West split became final: the churches of the West were Roman Catholic; the churches of the East were Greek Orthodox. The papacy went on to see its secular power reach its zenith. Then, reformers sought to correct the corruption of papal power, some within the church as orders of reform, and others on the outskirts of the church as the Waldensians, Wyclif, Hus, and Savonarola. The church had gained the world but lost its soul. The Holy Roman Empire and its Roman Catholic Church had become "the mother cesspool of immorality," as some of its own children declared, and ready for a thorough cleansing from heaven.

A.D. 590—Gregory the Great was made Pope of Rome

622—Islam was born at Mohammed's hegira

800—Charlemagne was crowned Holy Roman Emperor

988—Russia was "Christianized"

1054—The East-West split was completed

1095—The crusades began

1173—Waldensian movement, a preview of Protestantism, began

1208—Francis of Assisi forfeited his wealth for Christ's sake

1220—The Dominican Order was established

1232—The first "inquisitors" were appointed by Gregory IX

1272—Thomas Aquinas wrote his *Summa Theologiae*

1302—Papal supremacy was proclaimed by *Unam Sanctam*

1378—The great papal schism began

1380—Wyclif developed an English Bible translation

1415—John Hus was burned at the stake

1418—Thomas à Kempis wrote *The Imitation of Christ*

1453—The Eastern Roman Empire fell to Islam

1456—Gutenberg produced the first printed Bible

1479—The Spanish Inquisition was established

1497—The Church excommunicated Savonarola

1506—Work began on the new St. Peter's Cathedral in Rome for
    which money was raised across Europe by means of selling
    indulgences

The Reformation came to Europe on the tacks of a German Augustinian monk and priest by the name of Martin Luther, who had found true peace with God and conversion to a living Jesus Christ, not by following all the rules and stipulations of the Church, but by reading and believing what Paul had said in Romans about "justification by grace through faith." Luther discovered God's truth: faith alone, grace alone, Scripture alone, Christ alone; good works were to follow Christian faith. He rejected many of the evils of his contemporary Church, including the selling of indulgences (by which the Church gained money in exchange for an alleged forgiveness or "indulgence" for a sin people wished to commit some time in the future. This was a corruption of the concept of the grace and forgiveness of God; it was a scheme by which the medieval Church gained enormous wealth while ignoring the biblical call to all sinners to a holy life and an avoidance of sin). Luther's tacking his ninety-five statements to the cathedral door (the bulletin board of that day) was a normal thing for anyone to do who wished to enter into public debate about a matter; he had no idea that he would thereby start the greatest religious conflict in European history and eventually be ousted from the very Church he sought to help.

Soon many in Europe joined Luther in demanding that the Church clean up its act; among these was John Calvin, a French Catholic, scholar, and law student, who began to study the Scriptures and was converted to Christ and the Reformation. A writer of one of the world's greatest systematic theologies while still in his early twenties, he was forced to flee Paris in 1534 for safety in Geneva, in which city he performed most of his ministry and did his teaching to a generation of scholars in exile from around the world, including John Knox of Scotland. He reminded the world of biblical teaching on morals and ethics, government and personal responsibility; he developed a system of theology founded on the sovereignty of God and the priesthood of all believers; he provided the foundational concepts of republican, representative government for church and commonwealth. From Geneva, Calvinism permeated life and faith in Switzerland, France, the Rhineland of Germany, Holland, Hungary, Scotland and Northern Ireland, and parts of Eastern Europe and England, and wherever their colonists settled around the world, including America, where Calvinist Puritans arrived with the first English settlers in Jamestown in 1607!

> 1517—Luther tacked *Ninety-Five Theses* to the Wittenberg Cathedral door
>
> 1518—Ulrich Zwingli moved to Zurich, Switzerland
>
> 1525—The Anabaptist Movement began
>
> 1533—In Paris John Calvin was converted to the Reformation
>
> 1534—Henry VIII separated the English Church from Rome
>
> 1536—Calvin published his *Institutes of the Christian Religion*
>
> 1540—Loyola founded the Society of Jesus (Jesuits)

1545—The Counter-Reformation was initiated by the Council of Trent

1549—The Anglican *Book of Common Prayer* was distributed

1559—John Knox arrived on his final trip to Scotland

1563—The *Thirty-Nine Articles* was first published

1611—The *King James Bible* was published

1620—The *Mayflower Compact* was written

Calvinists settled America from many sources. The Dutch, who in 1623 settled New Amsterdam (New York), were Calvinists. The French Huguenots who settled the Carolinas were Calvinists. The Pilgrims and the Puritans held different forms of Calvinism while settling New England. Presbyterian Scots early settled in New Jersey and the Carolina coasts. Between 1705 and 1775 at least 500,000 Presbyterian Scotch-Irish came to America, primarily through Philadelphia, and then settled in western Pennsylvania and Ohio and in the mountains and valleys of inland Virginia, the Carolinas, Tennessee, and Kentucky, as well as Georgia and Alabama. By the time of the American Revolution, it is said that King George (blaming the rebellion on the Presbyterians) accused damsel America of being seduced by the Presbyterian parson!

There were enough Presbyterians in America by 1706 to form a presbytery and by 1716 to form a synod. The General Assembly was convened in Philadelphia in 1788, at which time our Presbyterian Constitution was written and the present republican and representative form of Presbyterian government was approved. Some of these same authors stayed in Philadelphia for the writing of the United States Constitution the next year. There is thus a close similarity of governance principles in these two documents and kinship between Presbyterian Church government and U.S. civil government. Presbyterians expanded rapidly by immigration and outreach; at one time it appeared as though Presbyterianism might actually become the largest Protestant family of faith in America. But in 1741, in 1837, and in 1861 schism set in, crippling an otherwise growing church. Resolutions to some of these controversies were only recently settled in 1983, though even that reunion caused some other negative separation in some local environments.

1633—Galileo was forced to recant his scientific theories

1636—Harvard College was founded to provide the New World with ministers

1646—The *Westminster Standards* were drafted in London

1678—John Bunyan wrote *Pilgrim's Progress*

1706—The first American presbytery was founded

1729—American Presbyterians adopted the *Westminster Confession/Catechisms* as "standard"

1732—The first Moravian missionaries were commissioned

1738—John and Charles Wesley experienced evangelical conversions

1740—The Great Awakening was at its height

1780—Robert Raikes began the modern Sunday School Movement

1788—The General Assembly of the Presbyterian Church, USA, was founded

1793—William Carey sailed for India and began the modern missionary movement

1801—American Congregationalists and Presbyterians adopted a "Plan of Union"

1806—In America the Cumberland Presbyterian Church was formed

1807—Wilberforce led in the abolition of the slave trade

1827—Darby founded the Plymouth Brethren and popularized dispensationalism

1837—American Presbyterianism divided into "Old School" and "New School"

1848—Karl Marx published *Communist Manifesto*

1855—Dwight L. Moody was converted to Christ

1859—Darwin published *On the Origin of Species*

1861—The American "Old School" Presbyterian Church
      divided North and South

1896—Billy Sunday began his revivals

1906—In America a partial reunion between the PCUSA and the
      CPC took place

1910—*The Fundamentals* were published and distributed to all pastors
      and leaders

1925—Modernists and Fundamentalists began a forty-year battle for
      control of the PCUSA

1929—The PCUSA Fundamentalists lost Princeton Seminary

1949—Billy Graham began his prominent career of Crusades for
      Christ

1973—The ultra-conservative Presbyterian Church in America was
      formed

1983—Mainline Presbyterians (North and South) reunited

In spite of controversy, the Presbyterian Church has faithfully
sought to spread the gospel to all parts of the world and, as 1995
General Assembly Moderator Marj Carpenter has discovered, has
founded more missions in more countries than any other denomination in history. The Presbyterian Church continues to make major
contributions to the worlds of education, law, science, business,
government, health, and peacemaking. The Presbyterian Church
offers a healthy environment in which to rear children in the Christian
faith, as parents know that they will gently be encouraged to
acknowledge a faith of their own at the appropriate time, a faith that
will carry them through the difficulties of life. The Presbyterian
Church is open, caring, committed to Christ, faithful to the Scripture,
and seeks to offer the world a Savior for our sin.

THE REFORMATION AND THE
MIDDLE WAY—*VIA MEDIA*

An Outline

I.   The Reformation and Presbyterianism

  A. The Renaissance
   1. Cultural Turmoil
   2. Political Turmoil
   3. Economic Changes in Western Europe
   4. Religious Change Developed into "The Reformation"

  B. The Three-Pronged Reformation (ca. 1500–1650)

   1. First Reformation of Luther (modest)
    a.) Form on Continent: Lutheranism (1517+) (successful in
        Germany and the Scandinavian countries and wherever
        their colonists settled)
    b.) Form in England: Anglicanism (1534+) (similar in mood
        to Lutheranism, but not directly related to Luther in
        leadership or cause for development) Successful in
        England and throughout the former British Empire
    c.) Discarded only those things explicitly forbidden in
        Scripture
   2. Second Reformation of Calvin, Zwingli (moderate)
    a.) Developed more thoroughgoing Reformation (1518+)
        (called variously "Calvinism," "Reformed Movement,"
        "Presbyterianism," "Puritanism")
    b.) Discarded both those things explicitly and implicitly
        forbidden in Scripture
    c.) Successful in Switzerland; France; Hungary; Holland;
        Scotland; parts of Germany, England, Poland,
        Czechoslovakia, Romania; and in many English, Dutch,
        and German-speaking areas of the world
   3. Third Reformation of Anabaptists (radical) (1525+)
    a.) Radical "Left" of Reformation: Mennonites, Baptists
    b.) Rejected anything tainted with Roman Catholicism,
        especially "Infant Baptism" and "Covenantal Theology"
        and "Churchianity"

        c.) Motto: "We speak where the Bible speaks; we are silent where the Bible is silent."

        d.) In America in early 1800s inspired Campbellite Movement (Disciples, Christians, Church of Christ)

    4. Counter-Reformation of the Roman Catholic Church (the Council of Trent, 1545)

II. *Via Media:* The Middle Way of Presbyterianism

    A. In Polity: Congregational, **Presbyterian**, Episcopal

    B. In Liturgy: Informalism, **Blend**, Formalism

    C. In Evangelism: Mass Evangelism, **Both**, Confirmation

    D. In Theology: Fundamentalism, **Balance**, Intellectualism

    E. In Freedom: Permissiveness, **Balance**, Authoritarianism

    F. Between Individualism and Churchianity: **Balanced Covenant Concept**

    G. Between Emotionalism and Rationalism: **A Faith of both Head and Heart**

    H. Blend of the best of the Continent and of the American Frontier

III. Presbyterianism: Its History and Meaning

    A. Moses and Jethro in the Wilderness (Exodus 18:13–27)

    B. History of "Elders"

    C. *Presbuteros* is Greek for "elder"

    D. Second largest group of Protestants in the world; Lutherans are first

    E. Double Standard: Broad in respect to membership; exacting (narrow) in respect to officers

    F. Origin of "Deacon": Acts 6:1–6

    G. God's Specifications for Officership: 1 Timothy 3:1–7; Titus 1:5–9; 1 Peter 5:1–4

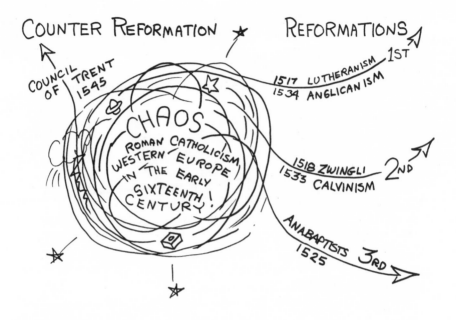

A Lecture

In the fifteenth and sixteenth centuries Western Europe arose from the deadness of the Dark Ages and threw off many of the shackles which had bound it for centuries. The Renaissance brought enlightenment in the arts, in education, in cultural revolution, and in mass change. Political turmoil saw the rise of nationalism and the sense of nationhood which marked the destruction of the Holy Roman Empire. Economic changes reintroduced the use of money, the rise of burghes and cities, the beginnings of the work ethic and the rise of a middle class, and the eventual demise of feudalism. Science was born; inquiry and learning again became respectable. With the printing press, literature was mass-produced for the scholars who multiplied and wrote and read in their native tongues as well as in the historic languages of Hebrew, Greek, and Latin. World trade expanded the West's knowledge of the earth. It is no wonder, then, that this sweeping expansion of knowledge soon troubled that ancient bastion of conservatism and what was contemporarily sometimes viewed as "the mother cesspool of immorality," the Roman Catholic Church (of that day)!

In the early sixteenth century, religiously speaking, chaos reigned in Western Europe and in the Holy Roman Empire, as religious change swept Europe when Martin Luther, John Calvin, and many others dared to challenge Rome on biblical grounds. (See the illustration on page 42.) Building on the witness of the early efforts for reform of the Roman Church by the Waldensians, Wyclif, Hus, Savonarola, and others, the Reformation was born in 1517 and kept Europe ablaze with change and controversy for 150 years; the world has never been the same since. Though sometimes we think of the Reformation as one continuing movement, it is truer to acknowledge that there were in the main three major Reformations, each succeeding upon the heels of the other, each producing a special kind of changed church.

If one assumes that the Roman Church was the "establishment" of 1517, the citadel of conservatism of that day, then the **First Reformation** (of Luther) was a purification which basically sought to redeem Rome or at least to limit the reform to a discarding only of those things (such as indulgences) explicitly forbidden in Scripture.

This was the thrust of Luther's efforts on the continent; out of this reform came Lutheranism. If the Roman Church had given just a little, it is highly probable that Luther would have remained Roman Catholic, as that was his original intention. He was forced out of the Roman Church and only reluctantly founded a new church.

In England in 1534, King Henry VIII sought only to break the political power of Rome, not to purify its ecclesiastical teachings, though reformation also eventually took place in England too. Thus, in England arose a second variant of Luther's modest reform; this has historically been known as Anglicanism/Episcopalianism, which more often than not bears a striking resemblance to a modified Romanism.

In both cases, much of the energy of each was invested in efforts to bring change within the Roman structure; failing that, each formed a new church much akin to the former. Even today it is clear that Lutheranism and Anglicanism retain much of the flavor of a right-wing, conservative evolutionary change from the "given" Roman mode.

After Luther came John Calvin, who, in 1533, centered his reform in Geneva, and who consciously sought a more thoroughgoing reformation. Calvin, supported by Zwingli, sought initially to stand with Luther in Luther's reformation; but when he could not agree with Luther on the true scriptural teaching regarding the Eucharist or the Lord's Supper, he went his own way and founded the "Reformed Movement." Calvin and his followers developed a more exacting reformation, discarding both those things explicitly forbidden in Scripture and those things which could be deduced as implicitly being forbidden by Scripture. Calvinism came to be known as "the Reformed Movement," "Presbyterianism," and in England "Puritanism." Calvinism significantly altered the religious map in Switzerland, France, Hungary, Holland, Scotland, in parts of Germany and England and eastern Europe, and flourished in most English-speaking and Dutch-speaking parts of the world, even up to today. Like the First Reformation, those in the **Second Reformation** sought to retain the biblical concepts of "catholic," as defining a "universal church" concept.

If "modest" describes the First Reformation, then "moderate" defines the Second Reformation. However, once the flames of change began to burn and the Scriptures were turned loose freely on the people, many alternative ideas surfaced. A **Third Reformation** took place, not led by one person nor contained in one area nor described under any one label other than "Anabaptist" (from the Greek prefix ana meaning "again"). This left wing of the Protestant Reformation turned radical and loosed all kinds of revolutionary forces and ideas. The Anabaptists rejected the concept of "universal church" or "catholic"; they rejected everything related to their former Roman attachments, including infant baptism and the covenant concept and "Churchianity." They supported only "believers' baptism" and were known as rebaptizers and cried bois-terously: "We speak where the Bible speaks; we are silent where the Bible is silent." These Anabaptists produced for the world those known as Mennonites and Baptists, and, later in America, the Campbellites (Christians, Disciples of Christ, and Church of Christ) followed in their train.

> Jack Rogers, formerly of Fuller Seminary, introduced me to part of the following illustrative analogy. As there were three strains of the Reformation, so there are three ways of cleaning out one's sock drawer: the Anglican/Episcopal/Lutheran way, the Presbyterian/Reformed way, and the Baptist/Campbellite way.
>
> The **Anglican/Episcopal/Lutheran** way is to open the sock drawer, perhaps half way, peek in, pull out those few obvious misfits and wornouts and quickly place them in the rubbish bin; one may then review the reformation, pronounce it "done," close the drawer, and go about other tasks. This is reformation modestly done!

The **Presbyterian/Reformed/Calvinist,** on the other hand, moves to the task with dispatch and determination, completely removing the sock drawer, turning it totally upside down on the bed; this reformer places a new paper liner in the drawer and then meticulously selects only the best and most useable socks in pairs to return to this "thoroughgoingly reformed" drawer, leaving all "questionables" out for immediate discard; the job has been done; only those items of which there is no doubt have been allowed to remain. This job has been well-reformed!

Finally, the **Anabaptist/Baptist/Church of Christ** approaches the same task with little enthusiasm; the reformer opens the sock drawer and with disgust on his face he calls a neighbor and together they haul the entire chest of drawers out of the house to the alley for city trash pick up, for in that sock drawer there was little to reform and a great deal to discard!

More could be said of the Reformation(s). Suffice it to be said that the Protestant Reformation produced three waves of reformation, distinctly different, with our Presbyterian heritage arising out of the *via media* of Protestantism. This remains true today and explains much of who we are and why we behave as we do.

Although followers of the Second Reformation could by no means claim exclusive rights to the following seven base or fundamental statements of belief, it is true that these theological cornerstones, taken together, uniquely formed Presbyterian thought:

1. The Lord God is the Sovereign Ruler of all things, all kingdoms, all people.
2. The Bible is God's Word to humankind and His "infallible rule for faith and practice."
3. All believers have direct access to God through His Son and therefore have the responsibility to serve as priests one to another.
4. God calls (elects) those whom He will in the context of the Covenant Community of Faith.
5. The Invisible Church of God is worldwide (catholic) in scope; breaks in the visible church obscure but do not destroy this essential unity of His Church, which is found wherever the Word is rightly preached, the sacraments are rightly celebrated, and church discipline is rightly administered.
6. The Lord Himself is the Lord of human conscience; no other human has the absolute right to dictate to another's conscience.
7. There should be zeal for righteousness but moderation in all things.

The people of the *via media* or middle way in every age, including our own, may be described as people ultimately orthodox in conviction and experience, but slow to force their views on others, even on other presbyters. We sense that everyone has a responsibility for his own views to answer to the Lord. We cringe at cutting others off. We trust God to rule and overrule, even in His Church. We may debate how to interpret Scripture, but ultimately we come out with a high view of Scripture and of the faith community, the Church.

We are broad, often adopting a latitudinarian posture toward others; this means that we often allow pluralism; sometimes too much for our own good. We are ecumenical to the core, even as we hold to our Reformed views. We are committed to a search for the unity of the Church, even as we seek ever to reform (by Scripture) our own Reformed Faith. We have never seen ourselves as the whole Body of Christ. We emphasize connectionalism as our way of declaring our opposition to independency. We struggle for one Reformed body per nation, which was Calvin's ideal. Even after we fight and split, we are conscience-bound to attempt to reconcile and to reunite. We are never content with where we are; we always struggle to attain a greater understanding and obedience of God's truth.

Ever pulled, ever pressed between independency (power to the masses) and hierarchy (power to the system), we press forward with a commitment to the middle way of representative government. We are the people of the *via media*, sometimes pulling friends from both left and right, while at other times losing people to those same left-right viewpoints. We provide an easy meeting place for persons from those other Reformations, but we find ourselves on occasion facing enormous tension in the left-right pull. All of these characteristics and tensions contributed to the long struggle for American Presbyterian reunion (1861–1983).

Let us look again at the Presbyterian Way, the *via media*.

A. **In polity (government)** Presbyterians are between the hierarchical system on the right and the congregational system on the left. Hierarchy, in either the oligarchy or monarchy forms, is comparable to the secular government of the few or of a king; congregationalism is the ecclesiastical form of the Greek city-state or the New England town-meeting. Presbyterianism is a republican form of government, akin to that of the United States of America, whose Constitution was greatly influenced by Presbyterians.

B. **In liturgy (worship)** we of the *via media* are not limited to high church formalism or low church emotionalism. We have room for heavy formalism with its read prayers; we equally are at home with informal worship with extemporaneous prayers and sermons from the heart, though well-prepared. We may or may not wear the academic gown, symbol of the teaching elder, or the clerical collar with tabs. There are few restrictions on laity's participation in worship leadership. We are a both/and blend in worship.

C. **In evangelism and church growth** we include room for mass evangelism and individual conversion. We normally grow our own Christians through the covenant family and the confirmation class, as young people take for themselves the vows first taken for them by their parents at their infant baptism. Yet, we also use the invitation for public profession of faith and receive many by adult profession of faith and baptism. We hold both revivals and preaching missions. We support church extension, new church development or planting, home and international missionaries, and rescue missions.

D. **In theology** the Presbyterian Church has always produced greater-than-normal-shares of great teachers and theologians. On the whole, we continue to be orthodox, by any standard. We are home to large numbers of fundamentalists who hold to a simple way of following the Lord of the Scripture. We also welcome those who would stretch our minds, inspire us with new insights into ancient truth, and provide intellectual stimulation of God's ever greater world. Presbyterianism at its best is balanced in this area; imbalance often produces for us problems which lead to splits and troubles within the family.

E. **In freedom** we seek to shelter pluralism with boundaries, broad boundaries. Just where to place those boundaries often causes strife. We permit people to hold diverse views within a Presbyterian framework. We even have a dual standard, requiring one level of assent to a general Presbyterian viewpoint by our ordinands (officers) and another level, quite broad, for our ordinary church members, who must declare themselves on five—and only five—constitutional questions (acknowledgment of one's personal sin; acceptance of God's Son, Jesus Christ, as one's personal Savior and Lord; agreement to attempt to live the Christian life; promise to support the Church family in its worship and work to the best of one's ability; and agreement to submit to the government and discipline of the Presbyterian system). All ordinands (deacons, elders, and ministers) must fit themselves generally within the Presbyterian theology and polity and pass examinations (both written and oral) by governing bodies of their peers. Hence, there is within the Presbyterian system both modified authoritarianism and modified freedom. Again, we see the middle way.

F. The people of the *via media* seek **a balance between individualism on the one hand and corporatism on the other.** We recognize every person as having two names: his/her given name describes one's uniqueness as an individual, created with no other copies by the heavenly Father and one who in a unique, unmatched way must be called to the Lord. On the other hand, each has a surname, symbolic of his/her belonging to a family, a family with whom God enters into covenant. Thus, Presbyterians believe in the covenant concept and emphasize the nurturing opportunity for God's Spirit to act and call.

G. We people of the middle way seek **to balance the human needs of emotionalism and rationalism.** We Presbyterians seek to commit to

God both our hearts and our heads. Presbyterians strongly support education for all; Presbyterians seek to help all the helpless through a strong sense of compassion.

H. History has blended into American Presbyterianism **the best of the continental experience of the Calvinists and the best of the American frontier,** particularly through the side history of the Cumberland Presbyterians, separate as a major body from 1806 to 1906. Among Protestants the world over we are the second largest body, with the Lutherans number one. George Gallup reports that of all religious groups in America today, we Presbyterians are the most evenly spread throughout all fifty states.

There are many obvious strengths to the heirs of the Second Reformation, not the least of which is the **compatibility** often furnished refugees from the First Reformation (high church people) or from the Third Reformation (low church people). In my own life I have personally been the beneficiary of such; this occurred when my English Anglican father and my American Southern Baptist mother found their greatest personal peace in service to God in the middle way of Presbyterianism.

Sam, a reserved Englishman, attended Mom's Southern Baptist services, only to find that not one, but every man, in the congregation had to greet him loudly, shake his hand, and pat him on the back, a most difficult experience for such a shy fellow. Then, when the services started there were much in-church visiting and talking, endless announcements, many crying babies, loud music directors, unknown emotional music, unscripted prayers, and a spellbinder of an extemporaneous and lengthy sermon with a never-ending demand at the invitation for souls to be saved that

moment, all of which conspired to make Sam a bit uncomfortable. Then, when he learned that his Anglican experience with Christ was just not acceptable to the Baptist Church, that he would have to repent of his sins (again), as though he had never been a Christian, become "a Baptist Christian," and be rebaptized by immersion, that was too much for him and quietly, but firmly, he told Lucile that he could not become a Baptist, no matter how much he loved her!

Lucile, an ardent and spirited Baptist of red hair and small stature, then determined that she and her groom would indeed worship together and form a Christian home even if she had to become an Episcopalian. Together they marched hand-in-hand the next Sunday to the Episcopal Church, where only a couple of gentleladies nodded a reluctant greeting and touched them with hands of gloved weakness. Unseen by most they slipped into a back pew where in near silence the service began with much kneeling and stately "collects" composed several centuries ago in King James English, heavy organ-overpowered hymns of unknown-to-Mom origin, an unenthusiastically-delivered intellectual lecture which failed to call anyone that day to any action for Jesus. His church was as quiet as hers was noisy. When she was finally able to obtain answers to her questions of inquiry, she discovered that she could be accepted as an Episcopalian once she had completed a course of study and the Bishop had visited to place his hand of approval on her. This did not set well with an action-now Southern Baptist.

Both disappointed in the other's church, this couple, as they continued their courtship, found the Presbyterian Church, which had enough noise, enthusiasm, and freedom for Mom and enough quiet and form and intellectual stimulation for Dad. Two weeks after their marriage they together became Presbyterians, these refugees from the First and Third Reformations having found the Second Reformation *via media*. I would also suggest with tongue-in-cheek their predestination became fulfilled that day! Thus, when the

Hassall children entered this world, we were welcomed into a single church family ready for us to worship as a family every time the church was open; how I do thank my parents for getting together in a single church prior to our entrance into the family! That decision molded my life for Christ.

My parents found that, whereas neither could accept the vast change to the other's Christian denomination, both could serve God in the somewhat compatible environment of the Presbyterian Church. Some of you have experienced this same phenomenon.

Another advantage is Presbyterians often are the **bridge people** between high church and low church. I remember that meeting of the Murfreesboro (Tennessee) Ministerial Association when I, as a Presbyterian, was able to enlist in our membership two friends, the local Roman Catholic priest and a neighbor Church of Christ minister/businessman. Have you not noticed that in most ecumenical groups Presbyterians usually surface to a higher percentage of top jobs than our numbers would ordinarily allow? In all my ministry I have noticed that I, a Presbyterian minister, have been one of the few persons who could normally be welcomed into any and every home of the community, for most persons feel they can at least partially relate to me and they knew that Presbyterian ministers do not normally take advantage of such hospitality to force their views upon unwilling neighbors.

There is a disadvantage to being of the Middle Way.

But, there is **one great disadvantage** to being of the middle way, a disadvantage which marks Presbyterian history as a series of explosions, "troubles," and schisms. Presbyterians seek to think for themselves and normally allow for diversity of opinion within their ranks. But every once in a while two sets of strongly-held convictions, often one set influenced from the left and the other influenced from the right, clash. The middle ground becomes a battlefield instead of a meeting ground. Of all groups the Presbyterians find the handling of such breaks the most difficult.

Baptists and other heirs of the Third Reformation with their non-centralized government divide over important issues like amoebas. The process is considered normative and occurs often enough to be survivable. Such divisions can often be healed quickly when divisive personalities leave. Such amoeba divisions have often actually become a means for reproduction and growth for such low church groups. On the other hand, the hierarchists apparently have discovered the means to retain symbolic unity in a pope, a council of bishops, a conference, a prayer book, or a centralized governmental system, while allowing for complete diversity within the body. We note that the Roman Catholics and the Episcopalians did not split during the U.S. Civil War. Usually in such hierarchical churches all local church property is owned by the centralized governmental authority. This tends to slow down schism.

Meanwhile, Presbyterians cannot divide like amoebas nor appeal to some centralized authority above the fray. Presbyterian polity requires a modicum of conformity to objective confessions. Alternative views may be examined by groups of peers who may declare a position as unacceptable, in spite of our heritage for pluralism. Presbyterianism seems to attract "partyism"; the "in's" often seek to force the "out's" out. Historically, those abandoning the Presbyterian vessel often found ways to take their property with them. Hence, the chief weakness of Presbyterianism is its inclination to split, to splinter, particularly in Scotland, America, and Korea. Presbyterians divide like splintering wood, splintering yet again. Yet, history shows that usually within three generations old wounds become new reconciliations.

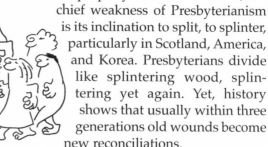

ETHOS AND PERSONALITY
OF THE PRESBYTERIAN CHURCH

But Joseph said to them [his brothers], "Don't be afraid. Am I in the place of God? You intended to harm me, but God intended it for good to accomplish what is now being done, the saving of many lives." (Genesis 50:19–20)

"Come now, let us reason together," says the Lord. "Though your sins are like scarlet, they shall be as white as snow; though they are red as crimson, they shall be like wool." (Isaiah 1:18)

Peter replied, "Repent and be baptized, every one of you, in the name of Jesus Christ for the forgiveness of your sins. And you will receive the gift of the Holy Spirit. The promise is for you and your children and for all who are far off—for all whom the Lord our God will call." (Acts 2:38–39)

In these three Scriptures we find clues to the emphases of Presbyterians and clues to our corporate character and personality, our "ethos" if you will.

In the Genesis reference we Presbyterians take great consolation that there is a Sovereign Lord of the Universe who has a plan and purpose for everything and makes sense out of all the chaos which surrounds us in our human existence. How good it is know that the One in whom we trust can take the worst that happens to us and bring good out of it, as Joseph discovered and as we observed with the cruel death of the innocent Jesus on the Cross! Indeed, if there is any one statement of truth which holds Presbyterians together and has become characteristic of us, it is the certainty of "the sovereignty of God" in and over human affairs.

In the Isaiah passage we find two balancing concepts which have become characteristics of those in the Presbyterian "Middle Way" family. There is first the assurance that the God who created humanity seeks "to reason" with us, to enable us to exercise our minds and to come to conclusions based on facts, and treats us (as creatures) as persons with whom He enjoys dialogue and conversation and relationship! Hence, those who check find Presbyterians particularly interested in the health of the human mind (along with education) and the exercise of reason (along with emotion) as each one discovers

God and God's way for us in our life of faith and practice. Secondly, there is clearly here emphasized God's concern both for the heinousness and pervasiveness of human sin along with God's delight in covering sin, burying sin, changing its nature and power over His beloved creatures who regularly fall and fail. Thus, there is here a balanced reference both to the reality of human sin and the power of God's redeeming grace. Again, we see foundational Presbyterian concerns which flower in our character.

In the Acts quotation from Peter's sermon at Pentecost we not only hear the clarion call for repentance (a Presbyterian emphasis) but also an assurance of the acceptance of sinners by Jesus Christ, of the promise of forgiveness, and of the certain gift of the Holy Spirit. We also hear Peter's plea that believers and their children be baptized and enjoy the promise of God. This promise of God (the covenant of the Old Testament now expanded by the death and resurrection of Jesus Christ) is not only for believers but for their children, not only for Jews but also for Gentiles ("those that are far off"). Although there are gratefully some of Jewish extraction who are members of our Presbyterian churches, most of us are Gentiles from the peoples who "are far off." Let us thank God for His expansive love to include us too in His plans.

Ethos is defined as "the distinguishing character or tone of a . . . religious group." Presbyterians, like all families of faith or denominations, have special characteristics which cluster among family members. I would propose that much of what is discovered to be characteristics which compose our unique ethos or personality arises out of two parallel sources: our place in history as heirs of the Second Reformation, or the *via media*, and our special Reformed theology. Just as the birth order of children within a family seems to have major influence on the developing characteristics of children when they become adults, so does our place in the development of the Protestant Reformation. We are the middle child of the Reformation.

One will generally find Presbyterians open to ideas from both left and right, high and low church, more formal and less formal, continental and American frontier, power flow from the top and power flow from the bottom, and able to relate positively both with fundamentalists and rationalists, and with colleagues from the Orthodox, Roman, Anglican, Lutheran, Anabaptist, Independent, and Bible Church traditions. Openness and variety characterize Presbyterianism.

The following series of words or phrases captures much of the "tone" of this "People of the Middle Way": "Reformed," "Calvinistic,"

"Presbyterian," "Connectionalism," and *Via Media.*

We hold what is called a "Reformed Theology," which is especially defined by its essential tenets with which we will deal in the next chapter (though most of these theological ideas have already come to our attention in the wording of the Five Church Vows we have previously reviewed).

"Calvinistic" refers to our specific heritage arising out of the teachings and practice of John Calvin, as he emphasized the authority of Scripture, God's sovereignty over all of life, human sin, God's grace, God's initiative, the power of the Cross, God's steadfastness, the priesthood of all believers, orderliness over chaos, involvement of the people in the governance of the Church, and the need to educate the mind, and to do all human vocation as unto God.

"Presbyterian" refers especially to "the rule of church life by lay elders and ministers" (both of whom bear the Greek label for "elder," which is *presbyter*), elected by the people and functioning in an orderly and graded series of governing bodies for the common good.

"Connectionalism" is the Presbyterian way of saying that, although we reject for our own use any hierarchical system (which places power at the top where such power simply flows down eventually to the people in a "trickle-down" design) or any congregational system (which may place all persons voting on all matters at all times, irrespective of their spiritual maturity and responsibility, and which may degenerate into a "rule by mob"), we firmly believe Christians are more effective and more biblical when we connect with each other and do not seek to live in isolation from each other. We reject the idea of an isolated Christian, for it seems to deny the valued *koinonia* or "fellowship of the saints," so highly lifted up in Scripture.

Via media Presbyterianism may be well and accurately defined by this series of seven couplets:

- a Biblical/Evangelical People
- a Reasonable/Moderate People
- an Ecumenical/Inclusive People
- a Compassionate/Caring People
- a Negotiating/Process People
- a Studying/Thinking People
- an Orthodox/Confessional People

Presbyterians of all perspectives claim the Bible as their authority. Presbyterians of all viewpoints declare good news for humankind; that is one meaning of *evangelical*. So, in a sense all Presbyterians can reasonably claim to be both biblical and evangelical. However, it must also be pointed out that most Presbyterians studied by the Presbyterian Panel, which is a Presbyterian Gallup Poll, are indeed biblical and evangelical in the more traditional sense of holding a high view of Scripture as the trustworthy Word of God and adhering to the essential uniqueness of God's only way of salvation through God's grace for sinful humanity in the atonement of Jesus Christ on the Cross.

By our history and by our theology Presbyterians have been led to place major emphasis on the value of human learning and competency in education for all. Presbyterians require their ministers to have graduate school educations and prove competent in human learning as well as in their theological studies. Presbyterians have always sought to found academies, colleges, and seminaries that all may know who God is and what God has provided humankind in the way of knowledge of our environment. The health and the use of the mind are critical to Presbyterians.

Being the middle child of the Reformation, Presbyterians early found that our views were "in-between" views, considered by many as too moderate. We would not be pressed into mediocrity nor into either a partial and lackadaisical reformation nor into a radical gang-busters all-or-nothing extremism. From our birth as a movement until today, it still is our nature to seek compromise, the middle road, the "let's all work together" approach. We therefore major on peacemaking, at least most of the time. Hence, a significant part of our self-image is that we are indeed reasonable and moderate people.

As a people who intentionally claim to be only a part of God's Church, it became incumbent upon us to reach out to others who are a legitimate part of God's Church; that includes all who truly believe in God's revelation of Himself as Trinity and who trust in God's incarnate Son as Savior from our sins and Lord of our

The Middle Child

lives. With these views foundational it is an easy matter to reach out to others who claim the name of Christ in fellowship and acceptance. Thus, Presbyterians accept the baptism of all other Christians when such baptism is done in the Trinitarian name of God and with water. Presbyterians accept the prior Christian experience and membership from most churches who claim Christ (there are questions about some few who appear to be more cultic than scriptural). Presbyterians have been in the forefront of almost all ecumenical movements. Presbyterians open our membership to all kinds of repentant sinners. Presbyterians generally have an "open-arms" policy towards other Christians around the world. We are ecumenical; we are inclusive.

Presbyterians, as Calvinists, are activists in almost all arenas of human need. We can be found in almost any trouble spot of the world, in almost any natural disaster or outbreak of disease. We care for the hurting and the dying in almost every environment. When we err, we tend to err in offering too much help or help in the wrong way, but we seldom err by having an uncaring spirit. Every General Assembly speaks as though it has authority in resolutions to solve most of the world's ills or conflicts that year; we sometimes know what we are doing. We always have the heart and the zeal; we do not always have the facts or the best solutions. But no one can accuse this People of the Middle Way of not caring, of not being compassionate.

John Calvin was trained in law and forensics, and much of his life he was both cleric and city manager. From that day to this those trained in law and in process seem very comfortable among Presbyterians. Our system of government does not allow us to acquiesce in the decisions made on high nor to agree to the demands of the throngs. Instead, we must negotiate, compromise, deal, perfect the nuances of language, and follow the process of legislation. Thus, we have a highly political heritage which requires us to perfect both the skills of negotiation and process. No wonder we make good leaders in business and government!

Our Latin motto is *Ecclesia Reformata, Semper Reformanda, Secundum Verbum Dei*, which means that we Presbyterians believe God has called us to be "The Church reformed, always reforming, according to the Word of God and the call of the Spirit." (This is vastly different from the erroneous view of some that we are to "change and always be changing.") The difference, of course, is the phrase "by the

Word of God and the call of the Spirit." In practice, this motto requires Presbyterians ever to be willing to review what Scripture says about any subject again and again. We are willing to study and restudy over and over again the same subjects, believing as we do that the Teacher of the Scripture, the Holy Spirit, always potentially has yet more to say to believing hearts and listening ears out of the same revealed Word of God available to us for centuries. Thus, we Presbyterians seek ever to be a studying people and a thinking people, using our God-given brains to go with our God-redeemed hearts.

Someone has said that if one throws a cat into the air, it will always land on its feet; since I have never tried this exercise, I will take this statement as truth. But, I do know that no matter how odd or unorthodox Presbyterians may appear at times, when all is said and done, we Presbyterians, like the cat, land on solid ground on orthodox feet. Our systems often move slowly, but they do move surely. God's way is ultimately discovered and supported by most Presbyterians most of the time. We also are a family of faith which writes down our convictions; indeed, we have a whole book of such written convictions, called "confessions, statements, creeds, catechisms, and declarations," which our ordinands must support in their ordination vows. Thus, the Presbyterian faith is not only orthodox (in the usual meaning of that word), but we are also confessional, meaning "true to our written statements of faith."

This People of the Middle Way are grace-filled, open, and inviting all seekers to discover Jesus Christ and walk with us in faith as we seek together to love and serve our Lord and Savior Jesus Christ. All believers are welcome to the family!

THE PRESBYTERIAN FAMILY CONNECTIONS

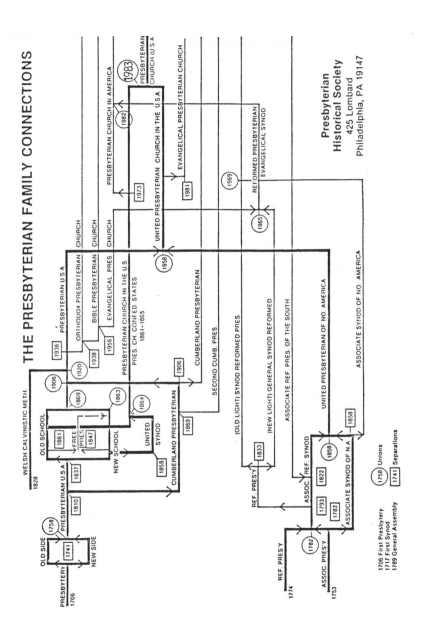

Presbyterian
Historical Society
425 Lombard
Philadelphia, PA 19147

SMALL GROUP DISCUSSION

A Word to the Leader

The above lecture on Presbyterian history and ethos should take no more than an hour of today's scheduled two-hour class. We recommend that at this point the group break into smaller groups, led by elders serving on the Session-appointed New Church Officer Training Committee, to spend fifteen minutes reviewing the seven basic theological cornerstones, found on page 46, and no more than ten more minutes formulating doctrinal or theological questions, for which the candidates have always wanted answers. Use a form, such as noted below. These questions should be gathered quickly and given to the leader to consolidate and to answer. This schedule leaves thirty minutes for the leader extemporaneously to seek to answer the questions offered.

PRESBYTERIAN DOCTRINE:
QUESTIONS I WOULD LIKE ANSWERED

1. _____

_____

_____

2. _____

_____

_____

3. _____

_____

_____

(Please hand to leader for answer.)

OUTLINE OF CLASS PRESENTATION

Question and Answer Time
Doctrinal/Theological Questions from Last Week

Lecture
1. "Introduction to Theology 101"
2. The Head of the Church
3. The Great Ends of the Church
4. Presbyterian *Confessions*
5. Essential Tenets of the Reformed Faith

Discussion
Church Discipline Questions and Answers

Summary of Essential Tenets
1. Trinity
2. Incarnation
3. Justification
4. Scripture
5. Sovereignty
6. Election
7. Covenant
8. Stewardship
9. Sin
10. Obedience

Homework for Session Four
1. Know Session III, pages 61–72
2. Read Session IV, pages 73–92.
3. Read "Form of Government," in the *Book of Order*.
4. Know the background of all confessions, pages 65–67.
5. Know "Essential Tenets of the Reformed Faith," pages 68–69.
6. Know "Presbyterian Discipline: Questions and Answers," pages 70–72.

INTRODUCTION TO THEOLOGY 101

In any such overview it is important to remember that "Reformed" refers to our theology, while "Presbyterian" denotes our government, a rule by elders (presbyters). We Presbyterians are children of Luther and Calvin and the sixteenth century Protestant Reformation; we sought, and continue to seek, to reform the church "by the Word of God." All Presbyterians should constantly seek to remain faithful to Scripture and to our heritage. We acknowledge there will be differences in emphasis and message between some within the same Presbyterian family; we are not all alike, but we do hold many common themes of faith.

The four basic questions with which theology deals are: (1) What is God like? (2) How has God revealed Himself to us? (3) What has God done for us? and (4) What does God expect us to do in response to Him?

The God of Scripture tells us who He is, for He has chosen to reveal Himself to us as the transcendent Creator and Originator of all things. He is above us and distinctly "other" than His creation. As creature, humankind is made in God's image and therefore can have fellowship with Him; we are capable of making moral decisions and acting responsibly. God has revealed Himself to us as Father, as Son, and as Holy Spirit, the Three-in-One, a difficult concept for any of us fully to understand. The Westminster Divines had it right when succinctly they said: "God is a Spirit, infinite, eternal, and unchangeable, in His being, wisdom, power, holiness, justice, goodness, and truth."

The first three methods of God's self-revelation are nature, conscience, and the Bible. In nature all may know that there is a God, who is good and almighty. Through human conscience we can understand something of "truth," "goodness," and "love," though all are terribly blurred both by original sin (the fall of our first parents) and by each individual's continued rebellion against God. Scripture is God's way of giving us greater evidence of His nature and His plan. When the human race still rejected this self-revealing God, He, in Jesus Christ, put on human flesh—Emmanuel—to dwell among us, to save us, and to bridge the gap between God and us. He made our redemption possible; that is, for those who believed Him.

In Jesus Christ God died for our sins and paid the penalty due us for our rebellion. Soteriology is the study of the Person and Work of Christ on our behalf. God, then, calls each to love Him, serve Him, and live His kind of self-giving life in the world for others, a sanctification in the here-and-now. Ethics is a call to live the godly life; missions is His charge to tell the whole world of His grace.

In the Protestant Reformation our forbears rediscovered four great truths: (1) Christ alone, (2) grace alone, (3) faith alone, and (4) Scripture alone; all are rebuttals to then-current Roman practices of a false dependence on good works, tradition, the mass, or the church for salvation. Presbyterians came to know that the Bible is "the only infallible rule for faith and practice"—the Bible is fully authoritative and is true in all the essentials—it teaches what we are to believe concerning God and what God expects us to do. Scripture is to be interpreted as it was originally meant to be interpreted, often literally, sometimes poetically or allegorically or eschatologically, with that which is clear explaining the obtuse.

Presbyterians understand "sin" as anything which separates us from God or keeps us from being or doing what God expects of us. The doctrine of total depravity makes it clear that there is no part of human nature uninfected with sin. Total depravity does not mean that we are all as bad as we can be, but that there is no part of our personality or nature that is not affected by sin. We also emphasize, even more strongly, God's grace, by which He saves lost humanity only through faith in the death of His Son for us on the Cross, an act of His freely giving of Himself for us. Salvation is by God's initiative, by God's grace, through Christ's work, for this Jesus was perfectly divine and perfectly human, yet without sin. He was sent from the Father and the Holy Spirit to be our Savior.

Presbyterians believe that God the Holy Spirit is the silent member of the Trinity; it is His task to uplift the Father and the Son. We believe that God from all eternity determined to call out to Himself a people, first Israel in the Old Testament, and then after the Cross, the Church, composed of believers of all generations and times, of all races and places. We Presbyterians are a part of God's true Church, not the whole of this covenant community of faith. God has called us to be members of the Church of Jesus Christ to obey Him through two sacraments: baptism (the water initiatory rite by which believers and their children are identified with Christ) and the Lord's Supper (the sustaining rite by which we regularly renew our covenant with Him by remembering the price of our salvation).

Reformed theology is not committed to any particular millennial view. However, we do believe that God initiated human history and will in His own time conclude this same history by the coming again of Jesus Christ in victory. We do not know when nor where this will occur. We believe our task is not to focus on the details of the end times, but to seek faithfully to accomplish His purpose on this earth by ministries both to the lost (evangelism) and the poor (justice).*

THE HEAD OF THE CHURCH

All power in heaven and earth is given to Jesus Christ by Almighty God, who raised Christ from the dead and set him above all the rule and authority, all power and dominion, and every name that is named, not only in this age but also in that which is to come. God has put all things under the Lordship of Jesus Christ and has made Christ Head of the Church, which is His body.

Christ calls the Church into being, giving it all that is necessary for its mission to the world, for its building up, and for its service to God. Christ is present with the Church in both Spirit and Word. It belongs to Christ alone to rule, to teach, to call, and to use the Church as he wills, exercising His authority by the ministry of women and men for the establishment and extension of His Kingdom.

Christ gives to His Church its faith and life, its unity and mission, its officers and ordinances. Insofar as Christ's will for the Church is set forth in Scripture, it is to be obeyed. In the worship and service of God and the government of the church, matters are to be ordered according to the Word by reason and sound judgment, under the guidance of the Holy Spirit.

In affirming with the earliest Christians that Jesus is Lord, the Church confesses that He is its hope and that the Church, as Christ's body, is bound to His authority and thus free to live in the lively, joyous reality of the grace of God.

(G-1.0100)

---

*This summary is based on the teaching of B. Clayton Bell Sr., to his church's officers-elect.

THE GREAT ENDS OF THE CHURCH

The great ends of the Church are:

the proclamation of the gospel for the salvation of humankind;
the shelter, nurture, and spiritual fellowship of the children of God;
the maintenance of divine worship;
the preservation of the truth;
the promotion of social righteousness; and
the exhibition of the Kingdom of Heaven to the world.

(G-1.0200)

PRESBYTERIAN *CONFESSIONS*

Presbyterians, like most Christians in church history, have found it exceedingly helpful to put our theology in writing and to support and adopt creeds and confessions (statements of faith) of Christians in other eras and places, if those meet scriptural standards. Thus, we Presbyterians have affirmed a book full of confessions, creeds, and catechisms from many ages and peoples. These are published and available for study in our *Book of Confessions*, a volume to which our ordinands (officers) must affirm support; ordinary members have no obligation to be led or guided by these, though the theology found in this book will appear in many sermons and in most of the suppositions underlying what is said and done in a Presbyterian church. Thus, in the Presbyterian Church, confessions indirectly impact the congregation, rather than directly. However, often portions of such will appear as "affirmations of faith" within our worship services. By such statements of faith ". . . the church declares to its members and to the world who and what it is, what it believes, and what it resolves to do" (G-2.0100a).

Within our *Book of Confessions* there are currently eleven documents. Below is a brief summary of each, its date, name, occasion, and key issues:

The Nicene Creed of the fourth century sought to clarify for all time certain key doctrines dealing with the person and work of Jesus Christ and the nature of the Trinity. It was the result of a conference called by the newly converted Roman Emperor Constantine who sought to reduce religious bickering and to develop a unified

Christian Church to bring greater cohesion to his Roman Empire.

The Apostles' Creed, the shortest document and the most popular, reflects second century baptismal statements, though all the ideas contained therein may be found in the sermons recorded in the New Testament. Actually formalized in the fifth century, the name indicates its intention to proclaim what the apostles themselves taught respecting the "essentials" regarding the Triune God and basic Christian dogma.

The Scots Confession of 1560 reflects the views of John Knox, who had recently returned from training in Geneva under John Calvin, in his efforts to lead Scotland out of the Romanism of Queen Mary and into the Protestant Reformation. This lengthy statement sought to clarify the biblical teachings its authors believed the Roman Church had rejected or misunderstood. It has special importance to Presbyterians.

The Heidelberg Catechism of 1563 reflects its German origin and its combined Lutheran and Reformed heritage. Requested by Freiderich III, the two Swiss reformers who authored this catechism (a question-and-answer rote memory method of learning) sought to lay out in plain language (for that day) the practical meaning of this reformed faith for daily living. There is a joy, a gratitude, and an uplifting spirit which still win modern supporters for its winsome theology and inspiring style.

In 1566 the Swiss Reformed Churches developed the *Second Helvetic Confession*, which provided much clarification in a confused day, especially about the Church and about the Christian experience of believers. Originally written as a personal statement of faith by Heinrich Bullinger, Zwingli's son-in-law and successor, this lengthy document noted both what to support and what to reject, biblically speaking.

The Westminster Confession and its sister documents, *The Larger Catechism* and *The Shorter Catechism*, were the results of four years of scholarly work by pious leaders in England in 1643–1646 as they daily gathered in Westminster Abbey, having been commissioned to develop a unifying faith-document for the Protestants of the British Isles by the Long Parliament. These doctrinal statements sought to deal systematically with the whole of Christian theology, basing its work on a strong commitment to Scripture, a high view of the sovereignty of God, and God's call to humankind through His covenant. These have proven to be the most influential creeds upon American Presbyterianism; as a boy I was privileged to obtain my personal theology by memorizing the *Westminster Shorter Catechism*. For serious Presbyterians I highly recommend Westminster and its magnificent teaching about Christian responsibility.

In 1934 *The Theological Declaration of Barmen* defied the Nazis and declared that these German Christians were prepared to die to put Jesus Christ before Hitler. The format was to declare what its authors supported and what they rejected as false doctrine or wicked actions.

Following the civil rights movement and anarchy in parts of America *The Confession of 1967* sought to explicate the theme and duty of reconciliation in a badly divided America. This modern creed, greatly influenced by neo-orthodoxy, caused much conflict and dissension before it was finally adopted by a then-liberal United Presbyterian Church in the United States of America, a product of a reunion between Northern Presbyterians and a branch of Scot Presbyterians in 1958.

A Brief Statement of Faith, adopted in 1991 by the PC(U.S.A.), was a promised by-product of the 1983 reunion between the Northern Presbyterians (UPCUSA) and the Southern Presbyterians (PCUS), which formed the PC(U.S.A.). It seeks in a few lines to provide an overview of contemporary Presbyterian faith which is both faithful to "the ten essential tenets of Reformed Faith" and inclusive of newer theological insights from Scripture. It does not cover all theological bases and does not claim to be comprehensive. This *Statement* may be found on pages 81–83 of this textbook.

The most important word everyone on earth must hear from *A Brief Statement of Faith* is "Yet" found in line 40—"Yet God acts with justice and mercy to redeem creation." This is the "Good News" that in spite of sin and condemnation, God loves God's creatures, including you and me! This is the heart of the Presbyterian understanding of faith!

ESSENTIAL TENETS
OF THE REFORMED FAITH

The Reformed Faith has certain characteristics and convictions without which it cannot exist; in other words, these convictions are essential for it to be what it claims to be; these "necessary convictions" are identified as ten "essential tenets." These are identified in our *Book of Order*, G-2.0300-2.0500.

The first two we share with Christians everywhere and in all time; thus, they are drawn from the "faith of the Church catholic": "the mystery of the triune God and the incarnation of the eternal Word of God in Jesus Christ."

  1. Trinity
  2. Incarnation

The next two we share with those who also were a part of the sixteenth century renewal of the Church: that is, from the faith and "affirmations of the Protestant Reformation"; "the rediscovery of God's grace in Jesus Christ as revealed in the Scriptures"; and "grace alone, faith alone, Scripture alone."

  3. Justification by grace through faith
  4. Scripture is the Word of God

The remaining six tenets are our family characteristics; as a family we hold the following from "the faith of the Reformed Tradition":

In its confessions, the Presbyterian Church (U.S.A.) expresses the faith of the Reformed tradition. Central to this tradition is the affirmation of the majesty, holiness, and providence of God who creates, sustains, rules, and redeems the world in the freedom of sovereign righteousness and love. Related to this central affirmation of God's sovereignty are other great themes of the Reformed tradition:

1. The election of the people of God for service as well as for salvation;
2. Covenant life marked by a disciplined concern for order in the church according to the Word of God;

3. A faithful stewardship that shuns ostentation and seeks proper use of the gifts of God's creation;
4. The recognition of the human tendency to idolatry and tyranny, which calls the people of God to work for the transformation of society by seeking justice and living in obedience to the Word of God.

G-2.0500(a);

5. Sovereignty of God;
6. Election;
7. God's involvement in the covenant community life;
8. Stewardship of our resources and the earth;
9. Sins of idolatry and tyranny; and
10. Commitment to justice and obedience.

Presbyterian Discipline:
Questions and Answers

1. **Where does one find the "Rules of Discipline" for the PC(U.S.A.)?**
   In the third section of the *Book of Order*.

2. **What are the five purposes of church discipline?**
   a. "To honor God by making clear the significance of membership in the body of Christ;
   b. To preserve the purity of the church;
   c. To correct or restrain wrongdoing in order to bring members to repentance and restoration;
   d. To restore the unity of the church by removing the causes of discord and division; and
   e. To secure the just, speedy, and economical determination of proceedings."

   D-1.0101

3. **How important are procedural safeguards in the exercise of church discipline?**
   It is the intention of the "Rules of Discipline" to provide in all respects and to all members procedural safeguards and due process.

4. **The power of Jesus Christ vested in His Church is for what purpose and how should it be exercised?**
   This power of Jesus Christ for discipline within His Church is "for the building up of the body of Christ, not for destroying it, and for redeeming, and not for punishing. It should be exercised as a dispensation of mercy and not of wrath so that the great ends of the church may be achieved. . . ."

   D-1.0102

5. **Church discipline is exercised within the context of pastoral care and oversight by means of administrative review. What does "administrative review" mean?**
   "Administrative review" is the supervision of lower governing bodies by higher governing bodies within the whole system of government of the church for the maintenance of its peace, unity, and purity.

6. **Church discipline is also exercised within the context of pastoral care and oversight by means of judicial process. What are the two kinds of "judicial process?"**

Judicial process is the exercise of authority by the governing bodies of the church for (1) the prevention and correction of irregularities and delinquencies by governing bodies, or by a council or any agency of the General Assembly—known as a remedial case; and (2) the prevention and correction of offenses by persons—known as disciplinary cases.

7. **How do the governing bodies of presbytery, synod, and General Assembly exercise discipline?**
   Through permanent judicial commissions which finally act for the governing body.

8. **How do sessions exercise discipline?**
   The session itself conducts trials.

9. **Define "an irregularity," "a delinquency," and "an offense."**
   "An irregularity" is an erroneous decision or action; "a delinquency" is an omission or failure to act; and "an offense" is any act or omission by a member or officer of the church that is contrary to Scripture or the Constitution of the PC(U.S.A.).

10. **Distinguish between "a dissent" and "a protest."**
    "A dissent" is an expression of disagreement with the action or decision of a governing body and is made during the meeting of that governing body. "A protest" is stronger; it is a written statement, supported by reasons, expressing disagreement with the action/decision of the governing body, a disagreement built on the conviction that that governing body has committed an irregularity or delinquency. If notice of a protest is given at that meeting of the governing body, it may be entered in writing later. If the protest is composed in a respectful manner, it may be entered in the body's minutes; the governing body has the right to enter a written response.

11. **What are "the general review" powers placed in the session?**
    The session has the right and obligation to review generally all the proceedings and actions of all committees, boards, and organizations in that particular church. Such an annual summary shall be incorporated in the session's minutes.

12. **Where may be found the rules for conducting administrative review and the two kinds of judicial process?**
    In "Rules of Discipline" in the *Book of Order*, as the third section.

13. **Name the degrees of church censure available to governing bodies in disciplinary cases.**
    In a disciplinary case the degrees of church censure are rebuke, temporary exclusion of ordained office or membership, and removal from ordained office or membership.

14. **Define "rebuke."**
    "Rebuke" is the lowest degree of censure for an offense, and consists of setting forth the character of the offense, together with reproof, which shall be pronounced along with prayer.

15. **Define the discipline of "temporary exclusion."**
    "Temporary exclusion" from the exercise of ordained office or membership is a higher degree of censure for a more aggravated offense and shall be for a definite period not to exceed two years. During this time, the offender must refrain from exercising any function of ordained office or, if a member, from any privileges afforded to church members.

16. **Define the highest degree of discipline which is "removal from office or membership."**
    "Removal from office" is the censure by which the offender's ordination and election are set aside, and the offender is removed from all offices without removal from membership.

17. **What is an "appeal?"**
    An "appeal" is the transfer to the next higher governing body of a remedial or disciplinary case, after judgment at the lower level has been rendered, for the purpose of obtaining a review of the proceedings and judgment to correct, modify, vacate, or reverse the proceedings and judgment.

18. **What four kinds of evidence may be presented to alter the degree of censure?**
    "If the accused is found guilty or after the guilty plea, the session or permanent judicial commission may hear evidence as to the extent of the injury suffered, mitigation, rehabilitation, and redemption. . . . The session or permanent judicial commission shall then meet privately to determine the degree of censure to be imposed."

                                                                    (D-11.0403e)

Outline of Class Presentation

Lecture
1. The Presbyterian Belief System
2. Five Points of Classic Calvinism
3. "The Presbyterian Church: Its Beliefs"
4. "The Reformed Faith . . . What Is It?"
5. "Thinking Like a Presbyterian"
6. The PC(U.S.A) *A Brief Statement of Faith*, 1991

Discussion

Presbyterian Doctrine Questions and Answers
The Sacraments

Homework for Session Five
1. Know Session IV, pages 73–92.
2. Read Session V, pages 93–109.
3. Read "Directory for Worship" and "The Rules of Discipline."
4. Know "Presbyterian Doctrine: Questions and Answers," pages 84–88.
5. Be familiar with *A Brief Statement of Faith*, pages 81–83.

THE PRESBYTERIAN BELIEF SYSTEM

One excellent way to discover the Presbyterian belief system is to review all the theological presuppositions contained within the questions used as the Five Church Vows, found on page 28. May I suggest five other avenues which may also provide insight into this goal.

Let us see what a brief review of the "five points of classic Calvinism," known as "TULIP," will teach us. Over four hundred years old, these are not broadly used today, but they do provide significant information regarding Presbyterian theological roots.

As we have seen on page 13, the *Book of Order* in its ordination vows provides an ordering by priority for spiritual authority which can save Presbyterian believers much grief and heartache by knowing what has top authority and what should draw our suspicions, lest we be entrapped by a Jim Jones or a David Koresh.

Our review of the ten "essential tenets of Reformed faith," as identified by our *Book of Order*, helped us understand what is uniformly important to those who hold a Presbyterian and Reformed theological perspective. Our overview on pages 40–58 gave us insights into the psyche of the people of the middle way.

In my personal experience of trying to understand Presbyterian theology and to explain Presbyterian beliefs, the tract, "The Presbyterian Church: Its Beliefs," by Ernest Trice Thompson, has been the most helpful; it is reprinted for the help it can offer to others in their search.

For those who want just a statement about the main difference between the Presbyterian Church and a specific other denomination, the reprinted article, "The Reformed Faith . . . What Is It," from *The Presbyterian Journal*, has proved of much assistance.

Five Points of Classic Calvinism

Total depravity teaches that all humankind is helpless before God due to human sin, which is resident in all areas and compartments of every human life. This doctrine does not hold that each person is as bad as he/she can be, but rather that all of us are infected with sin in every area of our lives. Thus, we humans utterly need God's intervention to save us from ourselves and our own choices.

Unconditional election declares that, no matter how we human beings get involved in the process of eternal salvation, clearly "God's choice of the sinner, not the sinner's choice of Christ, is the ultimate cause of salvation."* God is the only eligible voter in this election of eternity. How thankful we are that He chose us—and that not of our doing but out of His grace and for our serving!

Limited atonement denotes that the Cross of Calvary was adequate to cover the penalty due for the sins of those whom God in Christ determined to save. Its further teaching that the Cross was efficacious for those saved, and them alone, is less accepted by today's Presbyterians than these other teachings. Ben Rose seeks to clarify the meaning of this doctrine by saying: ". . . Christ's sacrificial death on the cross—His atonement—was and is specific, limited, and effective. It was specifically designed for and limited to those whom the Father had given the Son; and it effectively accomplished their salvation."**

Irresistible grace declares that God's grace "never fails" and is therefore "invincible." God in Christ through the Holy Spirit "graciously causes the elect sinner to cooperate, to believe, to repent, to come freely and willingly to Christ."*** God's goodness fulfills His desire to save those whom He has chosen.

Perseverance of the saints is a theological way of saying that God never loses those who are His. He is always faithful and does not and will not let those who are His children slip out of His hand; His patience in loving us to the end is beyond understanding but such a joy for those who experience this "assurance of salvation."

---

* David N. Steele and Curtis C. Thomas, *The Five Points of Calvinism Defined, Defended, Documented*, Presbyterian and Reformed Publishing Co., Philadelphia, 1963, p. 17.
** Ben Lacy Rose, *T.U.L.I.P.: Sermons on the Five Points of Calvinism*, Providence House Publishers, Franklin, TN, 1992, p. 39.
*** Steele and Thomas, op. cit., p. 18.

"THE PRESBYTERIAN CHURCH: ITS BELIEFS"

Ernest Trice Thompson

The Presbyterian Church has definite beliefs, drawn directly from the Word of God, which are stated clearly. It holds the common Christian faith and cooperates fully with all other Christian people. Some of its important beliefs are summarized briefly in the paragraphs that follow:

God—God, the Creator of the heaven and the earth (Genesis 1:1) is Sovereign Lord of the universe (Daniel 4:35). He has revealed himself partially through nature and fully in the Bible. His supreme revelation of himself is in Jesus Christ. God is righteous in all his ways, loving in all his dealings (2 Peter 3:9).

Man/[woman]—Man/[woman] is a sinner, unable to save himself/(herself), and therefore needs a Savior (Genesis 6:5–6; Romans 3:19–23; Romans 6:23a).

Christ—God, out of his great love, provided a Savior (John 3:16–17). This one and only Savior is the Lord Jesus Christ, God's own Son, born of a woman, and is therefore God and man, and as such is able to make reconciliation between God and man/(woman) (Romans 3:24–26).

Salvation—For our sin Christ died on the cross, taking upon himself our guilt and the penalty of sin that we might be forgiven and set free (Romans 5:8; 8:1).

Faith—Salvation comes to us only through our faith in Jesus Christ as Savior and Lord (Romans 6:23; Ephesians 2:8–9; John 1:12; John 3:14–15; Acts 16:30–31; Hebrews 7:25).

Repentance—Repentance from sin, which is more than sorrow for sin, is a turning away from sin unto newness of life in Christ (Mark 1:14–15; Acts 2:37–38; Matthew 3:8).

The Holy Spirit—The Holy Spirit leads to conviction of sin, to repentance and faith, and to a desire for a new life, and so brings about the new birth without which no man/(woman) can enter into the Kingdom of Heaven; and He enables us to die more and more unto sin and to live more and more unto righteousness (John 3:3–8; John 16:7–13).

The Bible—The Bible is the inspired and authoritative Word of God (2 Peter 1:19–21; 2 Timothy 3:16).

The Organized Church—The organized church is a divine institution for the worship of God, the propagation of the faith, and the mutual comfort and strength of those who believe (Matthew 16:16–18; Ephesians 5:23–27).

The Sacraments—There are only two of these holy ordinances instituted by Christ, wherein by outward signs, inward spiritual meanings and graces are conveyed to sincere participants—worthy receivers.

> **Baptism**—Water baptism, a symbol of spiritual baptism, is the rite of entrance into the church; it is to be administered to all who believe in Christ and to their children as a token that they are members of the household of God (Acts 16:14–15; Ephesians 6:4; Acts 16:32–33).
>
> **The Lord's Supper**—This is a memorial of Christ's life and death and coming again (1 Corinthians 11:23–26).

A Public Confession of Christ as Savior—A public confession of Christ as Savior is made by joining the church (Matthew 10:32).

The Lord's Day—The first day of the week is the Christian Sabbath for public worship. After the resurrection of Christ the disciples met for prayer and worship on the first day of the week (1 Corinthians 16:1–2; John 20:19–26).

Christian Responsibility for Witnessing for Christ—A Christian has the responsibility of witnessing for Christ, and so helping to build up a human society permeated by the spirit of Christ (Acts 1:8; John 1:34–42; 2 Corinthians 3:2–3).

The Bodily Resurrection of Christ—The resurrection of Christ was a bodily resurrection. There will also be a bodily resurrection of all men/(women) and recognition in life to come (1 Corinthians 15:3–4, 20–23; John 14:1–3).

The Second Coming of Christ—The second coming of Christ will be personal and glorious. It is ours to watch and work and be ready when He comes (Matthew 24:42-44).

The Final Judgment—There will be final judgment with Christ as the Judge; and there will be eternal blessedness for all those who in this life accept Jesus Christ as Savior and seek to follow Him as their Lord (Acts 10:42; Hebrews 9:27; 2 Corinthians 5:10).

"REFORMED FAITH . . . WHAT IS IT?"

(Copied from The Presbyterian Journal, *October 4, 1972)*

A thoughtful church member asked her pastor: "What is the *Reformed Faith* to which you so frequently refer? I hear much of the *distinctives of the Reformed Faith* without a clear indication as to what those distinctives are."

Below is a paraphrase of the answer the pastor gave:

The Reformed Christian believes that he/she is justified by faith in Jesus Christ through the immediate work of the Holy Spirit in his/her heart, hence he/she is *not a Roman Catholic.*

The Reformed Christian believes in the Trinity, therefore, in the full deity of the Lord Jesus Christ, so he/she is *not a Unitarian.*

The Reformed Christian believes in the sacraments and the Word of God as means of grace, so he/she is *not a Quaker.*

The Reformed Christian believes in a prior work of God's grace in the human heart leading to salvation, and in the predestination of all things according to God's sovereignty, so he/she *isn't a Methodist.*

The Reformed Christian believes that the priesthood of all believers has replaced a special priesthood, and that ordination is by the Holy Spirit and not by any power granted in human succession, so he/she *isn't an Episcopalian.*

The Reformed Christian believes that baptism represents the coming of the Holy Spirit upon the believer, and that the promise is to believers and to their children who are also heirs of the covenant, so he/she *isn't a Baptist.*

The Reformed Christian believes in a representative government rather than a purely democratic government, so he/she *isn't a Congregationalist.*

In addition to these denominational distinctives, *the Reformed Christian* bases his/her relation to God and his/her hope of salvation on the gospel of the Lord Jesus Christ, incarnate Son of God, crucified for our sins, raised for our justification, reigning in the hearts of His people by the Holy Spirit, and coming again in time to judge the quick and the dead.

He/she also believes in the fellowship of believers on earth and in fruitful Christian living.

"THINKING LIKE A PRESBYTERIAN"

Many years ago Joseph Gettys provided the PCUS with an invaluable booklet, *Meet Your Church*, to encourage inquirers into Presbyterian membership. One particular chapter, "Thinking Like a Presbyterian," made a significant impression on me and a few of its major ideas cannot be improved upon and deserve passing on to a new generation of would-be Presbyterians. I hold that there is a distinct Presbyterian way of "seeing life"; this Presbyterian character is formed by our theology, our history, and our ethos. It is an honorable way of enjoying faith and pleasantly serving the Lord.

We start our "thinking with the Bible as our guide." Whatever is the challenge before us, whatever we seek to do in life, whatever problem lies before us, we Presbyterians find it a natural habit early on to turn to Scripture to discover what God says which may be of help to us in our time of challenge, confusion, or crisis. We understand that God's Holy Spirit is ever seeking to teach us what God's will is for our circumstances; Scripture is His first means of communicating with us.

We know instinctively that God is in charge, that God already knows what is happening and what the conclusion will be, and that God will bring good out of it, no matter how bad it may initially appear from our human viewpoint. We know our first and foremost task in this life is "to glorify God and to enjoy Him forever." We continue "thinking with God at the center of life." This keeps us from becoming self-centered or focused on our own problems, sins, or failures. When we know the Father is the captain of the vessel, the sea storms seem less frightening. When we remember that the Creator of the Universe is our own personal "Abba," "Daddy," then we fear even the worst devils and fiercest creatures no more. We have been gifted with the comforting assurance that we are held in the hollow of His hand, that "He cares for us." What joy to know that "in life and in death we belong to God" and that "with believers in every time and place, we rejoice that nothing in life or in death can separate us from the love of God in Christ Jesus our Lord!"

As we Presbyterian believers journey through life, we are reminded that we are to "keep Christ and the Holy Spirit as living realities." We know God's mercy, but we experience Him firsthand through Jesus Christ; later we come to know God as the Comforter, the shy Person of the Trinity, Who never calls attention to Himself but always seeks to place the spotlight on Jesus. Presbyterians do not easily go off on tangents into "Jesus Only" or "Holy Ghost" extremes; we simply daily plod along happily knowing that God, the Triune One, wants us to have no wobbles in our balanced relationship with the Trinity. We know that Jesus saves us and that the Holy Spirit is personal, present, and empowering us daily for God's good and glory.

As we live, it is important to Presbyterians to remember that in this life we can never become perfect; nor are we called to be "Messiah" to anyone else. Thus, we seek to "keep sin and salvation in our doctrine of redemption." Sin is not simply a past dragon once slain; sin is a nipping dog at our heels, alive and far too active in our lives. We Presbyterians know we never outgrow temptation and can always fall, so we attempt to cultivate a humble spirit both about our own potential for renewed failure and our neighbor's imperfections. However, we seek to keep ever before our eyes the assurance of God's salvation in Jesus Christ, Who on the tree did redeem unworthy folk like ourselves! Friends, this is both a healthy and a humble theological reality.

Presbyterians know our salvation comes from the Lord, that He took the initiative, that we are saved by His grace through our faith (which He provided). We have been taught the difference between what is the root of faith (salvation) and what is the fruit of faith (our good works). Therefore, we find it necessary to "keep the proper relationship between faith and works." Having been saved by His grace, we know our task is to produce for His glory a garden of the fruit of good works and pleasant blessings for others, all that the Father may be honored!

As maturing Presbyterian Christians, we have come to understand how important it is to worship God regularly both at home and in the sanctuary and to offer Him the gift of service to our fellow human beings, especially to those less fortunate than we. Thus, we do seek "to keep worship and work as spiritual twins." We have discovered that the best place ordinarily for Christians to grow is in God's Church; we remember "to keep the Church as the instrument of God" here on earth meant for our good and

Thinking like a Presbyterian.   maturity in Christ.

A BRIEF STATEMENT OF FAITH (1991)
PRESBYTERIAN CHURCH (U.S.A.)

In the ensuing pages we quote the text of this latest confession and in **bold print** note at least ten biblical ideas new to confessions, as well as list the line numbers where the essential tenets may be found. As a member of the final writing team for this confession, I have strong convictions that this statement is both true to Scripture and true to where Presbyterians are today in our theology. An oral reading leaves one feeling the faith, the power, and the integrity of those holding such views in a world of uncertainty, moral confusion, and human need.

[Let us now read this statement of faith in unison.]

1 In life and in death we belong to God.
2   Through the grace of our Lord Jesus Christ,
3   the love of God,
4   and the communion of the Holy Spirit,
5   we trust in the one triune God, the Holy One of Israel,
6   whom alone we worship and serve.

7 We trust in Jesus Christ,
8   **fully human, fully God**.
9   Jesus **proclaimed** the reign of God:
10   **preaching** good news to the poor
11   and release to the captives,
12   **teaching** by word and deed
13   and **blessing the children**,
14   **healing** the sick
15   and **binding up** the brokenhearted,
16   **eating** with outcasts,
17   **forgiving** sinners,
18   and **calling** all to repent and believe the gospel.
19   Unjustly condemned for blasphemy and sedition,
20   Jesus was crucified,
21   suffering the depths of human pain
22   and giving his life for the sins of the world.
23   God raised this Jesus from the dead,

24   vindicating his sinless life,
25   breaking the power of sin and evil,
26   delivering us from death to life eternal.

27 We trust in God,
28   whom Jesus called Abba, Father.
29   In sovereign love God created the world good
30   and **makes everyone equally in God's image,**
31   **male and female, of every race and people**
32   **to live as one community.**
33   But we rebel against God; **we hide from our Creator.**
34   Ignoring God's commandments,
35   we violate the image of God in others and ourselves,
36   accept lies as truth,
37   exploit neighbor and nature,
38   and **threaten death to the planet entrusted to our care.**
39   We deserve God's condemnation.
40   Yet God acts with justice and mercy to redeem creation.
41   In everlasting love,
42   the God of Abraham **and Sarah** chose a covenant people
43   to bless all families of the earth.
44   Hearing their cry,
45   God delivered the children of Israel
46   from the house of bondage.
47   Loving us still,
48   God makes us heirs with Christ of the covenant.
49   **Like a mother who will not forsake her nursing child,**
50   like a father who runs to welcome the prodigal home,
51   God is faithful still.

52 We trust in God the Holy Spirit,
53   everywhere the giver and renewer of life.
54   The Spirit justifies us by grace through faith,
55   **sets us free to accept ourselves** and to love God and neighbor,
56   and binds us together with all believers
57   in the one body of Christ, the Church.
58   The same Spirit
59   who inspired the prophets and apostles
60   rules our faith and life in Christ through Scripture,
61   engages us through the Word proclaimed,

62   claims us in the waters of baptism,
63   feeds us with the bread of life and the cup of salvation,
64   and **calls women** and men to all ministries of the Church.
65 In a broken and fearful world
66 The Spirit gives us courage
67   to pray without ceasing,
68   to witness **among all peoples** to Christ as Lord and Savior,
69   **to unmask idolatries in Church and culture,**
70   **to hear the voices of peoples long silenced,**
71   **and to work with others for justice, freedom, and peace.**
72 In gratitude to God, empowered by the Spirit,
73   we strive to serve Christ in our daily tasks
74   and to live holy and joyful lives,
75   even as we watch for God's new heaven and new earth,
76   praying, "Come, Lord Jesus!"

77 With believers in every time and place,
78   we rejoice that nothing in life or in death
79   can separate us from the love of God in Christ Jesus our Lord.

80 Glory be to the Father, and to the Son, and to the Holy Spirit. Amen.*

LOCATION (BY LINE) OF "ESSENTIAL TENETS"

Trinity	5–6, 7–27–52
Incarnation	8
Justification	54
Scripture	58–61
Sovereignty	29, 40
Election	41–43
Covenant	47–48
Stewardship	37–38
Sin	33–38
Obedience	69–71, 73–74

---

* Instead of saying this line, congregations may wish to sing a version of the "Gloria."

PRESBYTERIAN DOCTRINE:
QUESTIONS AND ANSWERS

1. **What is involved in Vow 1 respecting one's faith in Jesus Christ?**
    It is clearly expected that every ordinand be a believing Christian, one who personally knows Jesus Christ as Savior and Lord and who seeks to follow Him in life and who has experienced the full Godhead of the Trinity: Father, Son, and Holy Spirit.

2. **How are Presbyterian ordinands expected to view Scripture?**
    It is clear that the Presbyterian ordinand is to accept the full Bible as God's Word, nothing less; the Bible, then, is God's Word by the power of the Holy Spirit. The Bible is absolutely one-of-a-kind with total and complete authority in its trustworthy message, revealing to a lost world our Savior, the Lord Jesus Christ. Other confessions add that the Bible is our only infallible rule for faith and practice.

3. **Rank the spiritual authorities over our lives, by virtue of our vows.**
    Primary authority is Jesus Christ, the Living Word; secondary authority is the Bible, the Written Word, as revealed through the Holy Spirit; tertiary authority is the "essential tenets of the Reformed faith," as found in our Presbyterian confessions; the fourth authority is the combined testimony and experience of the church, especially as determined by actions of governing bodies; and the fifth authority is the personal understanding and experience of the individual Christian.

4. **Who determines what the "essential tenets of the Reformed faith" are in respect to acceptance/rejection of a potential ordinand?**
    The governing body of original jurisdiction so determines in each case. This means the session for deacons and elders and presbytery for ministers. This determination is always open to the process of review by the higher governing bodies, under the process of appeal or complaint.

5. **What is involved in "receiving and adopting the essential tenets of the Reformed faith as expressed in the confessions of the church . . ."?**
    This acceptance of the plain teachings of our confessions must be sincere, personal, knowledgeable, active, and wholehearted, but such does not necessarily involve total acceptance of every detail and minutia. There must be an appreciation, understanding, and

acceptance of the major concepts and essential tenets, teachings, viewpoints, and distinctive dogmas contained herein.

6. **Describe the Presbyterian system of doctrine.**

The Presbyterian system of doctrine is Scriptural, Protestant, Evangelical, and Calvinistic by intent. "Presbyterians do not hold that all other interpretations of Scripture are so wrong as to rule out of the Church those groups or individuals who adhere to them." (Kenneth J. Foreman Sr.)

7. **What are the five rival systems of doctrine to the Calvinistic system?**

The rivals of Calvinism are:

a. Scholasticism of the Roman Church;

b. Traditionalism of the Orthodox Churches;

c. Socinianism of the Unitarians and Modernists;

d. Arminianism of the Methodist and Holiness Churches; and

e. Any of a number of varieties of cults, arising out of the Protestant radical fringe: Mormons, Jehovah's Witnesses, Eddyism, Unity, etc.

8. **Point out the most serious weakness in the rationale of each of these five rival systems.**

Scholasticism is overly dependent upon the Sacraments and too often deteriorates into a "works-righteousness" religion. Traditionalism is overly dependent upon the traditions of the Eastern Church, particularly through the eleventh century. Tradition seems to crowd out Scripture as the final arbiter of disputes. Socinianism is so overly dependent upon human reason that it often discounts the supernatural to the extent of crowning man/woman and "reason" in the place of God; it thus often succumbs to another "works-righteousness" religion. Arminianism tends to be overly dependent on human free will. Cults are overly dependent upon extra-biblical sources and the personal visions and divine confrontations of their human leaders.

9. **What do the Scriptures principally teach?**

"The Scriptures principally teach what man (woman) is to believe concerning God and what duty God requires of man (woman)." *Westminster Shorter Catechism* #3.

10. **Who is Jesus and what did He do?**

Jesus Christ is the God-man sent to save the world from their sins. Jesus Christ was born of a virgin, as plainly revealed in Scripture. He is the Word made flesh. He is absolutely divine. His purpose in being born in a state of humiliation was that He might give His life as a ransom for many. He came to die in the place of sinners. The Bible teaches that Jesus substituted His life for ours on Calvary. Christianity is a religion of blood, the blood of Jesus Christ through which and by which the sins of believers are washed away. The preaching of the Cross as the only way of salvation is foolishness to the world, but it is the power of God to the sincere servant of God.

11. **What is sin?**

"Sin is any want of conformity unto, or transgression of, the law of God." (WSC #14)

12. **What is man's/woman's chief end?**

"Man's (woman's) chief end is to glorify God and to enjoy Him forever." (WSC #1)

13. **What is it to repent?**

To repent is to be sorry for sin, and to hate and forsake it because it is displeasing to God. (See WCF, SVII:6)

14. **Do good works save?**

Though the moral law is binding upon both Christian and non-Christian, it is never the means of justification, which is an act of God's free grace.

15. **If you should die tonight and enter into the presence of your Maker, why should He allow you into enter His Heaven?**

Not because of anything I have done or not done; not because of my church membership, my moral conduct, my good works; not because I am an officer of the Presbyterian Church and sought to serve Him while I was on earth; but because I trusted in the shed blood of Jesus Christ, Whom by faith and through His grace I accepted as my Savior and Lord, in spite of my personal unworthiness.

16. **What are the sacraments?**

Baptism and the Lord's Supper.

17. **What is the duty which God requires of man/woman?**

"The duty which God requireth of man, is, obedience to His revealed will." (WSC #39)

18. **Do Presbyterians believe that Jesus literally rose from the dead?**
Most assuredly Presbyterians proclaim with vigor the physical resurrection of Jesus Christ, as He overcame the grave, death, and sin, and all the powers of Satan. Because He arose, we too are assured of our resurrection to be with Him forever. The doctrine of the resurrection is the keystone of the Christian theology. (1 Corinthians 15:12–19)

19. **Do Presbyterians believe in "total depravity"?**
Yes, the total depravity of man/woman is recognized as true, despite the false brightness of modern humanism. This does not mean that all men/women are as bad as they can possibly be, but it does mean that man/woman is "defiled in all the faculties and parts of soul and body." (*WCF*, VI:2)

20. **How important is the Church to Presbyterians?**
Presbyterians recognize the Church as an instrument of God in this age, an imperfect instrument to be sure, but one blessed by God. The Church is found wherever God's people meet to hear His Word properly preached and to celebrate His sacraments properly. But, the Church always stands under the judgment of the ultimate authority, the Holy Scripture, and therefore is ever in need of reformation.

21. **What do Presbyterians believe about the Christian life?**
Presbyterians should teach and provide a living example of the Christian life of purity. The saints—God's called-out people—should live as saints of God everywhere. Their lives should be distinctive and different. Their values and goals in life should be peculiarly above those of the world. Ultimately, the test of purity of life is the test of one's beliefs. The orthodox Christian is the Christian with the clean life, one following in the steps of the Master.

22. **What is the mission of the Presbyterian Christian and how does he/she enter into mission?**
He/she, convinced of his/her own call from God and committed to God's Word, seeks to move out into the world in mission both to "the lost" and to "the poor" in twin ministries of evangelism and justice, both as a part of his/her church life and as a part of his/her witness in the world of work, school, or recreation. Stewardship of all of one's resources—times, talent, treasure—is an obvious result of one's call to a life of Christian commitment.

23. **What do Presbyterians mean when they affirm God's predestination?**

Presbyterians reject the deterministic philosophy of "what will be, will be," but they cheerfully affirm "what God wills, will be!" "We believe that God has a plan for His universe and for every man/woman and nation involved. We are sure that His plans are made for good and helpful purposes. We are taught that God from all eternity chose certain people to be saved and that in His Own time and way He provides the needful means of salvation. No one is chosen because he/she is worthy or good enough, but only because God gives to him/her unmerited grace and love. Though Christ dies for all and offers His redemption to all, the condition of receiving it is faith. Those who refuse to meet the condition cannot accept the gift." (John 3:16)

24. **Explain the difference between "the visible church" and "the invisible church."**

"The visible church" is how we describe the particular congregations and denominations, as seen by the human eye as they function as human organizations. "The invisible church" refers to the one true church as seen by God Himself and is composed of true believers in every age, in every visible church, in numerous human institutions.

25. **Briefly describe how you would tell an inquirer how he/she might "be saved."**

Select your own way of expressing the biblical truth that salvation comes only through Jesus Christ. A simple, though effective, way is to emphasize these three aspects of faith:

a. Repent of one's sins (that is, turning away from what displeases God);

b. Believe in(to) Jesus Christ (that is, commit one's life into the personal responsibility of Jesus Christ, as He is offered in the Bible); and

c. Accept God's gift into one's heart as Lord (that is, freely to unwrap God's gift of the Savior and deliberately enthrone Him as Lord in one's heart, immediately seeking to give Him obedience).

Such a process of repenting, believing, and accepting changes the believer into a follower of Jesus Christ, which at the same time is the simplest and most profound description of a Christian.

THE SACRAMENTS

Presbyterians, like Protestants the world over, hold there are but two sacraments, believing that a sacrament is an instruction from Jesus Christ to all His followers in which He commanded us to do a particular action (which is visible for all to see) which has a deep hidden and invisible spiritual meaning. Only baptism and Communion, or the Eucharist, fulfill this definition, in our view.

A. The Lord's Supper or Eucharist or Communion. There are at least four ways to view the Lord's Supper:

1. The Roman Catholic Church teaches "transubstantiation." This view holds that the elements of bread and wine actually become the body and blood of our Lord Jesus Christ, even though these changes remain unseen and unproven by science. This is a faith view. It also alters the way we handle the elements, view the Supper, and conduct our life around what comes then to be known as "the mass." Presbyterians do not hold this view.

2. The Lutheran Church has altered this view a bit, but from our Reformed viewpoint, not enough. Lutherans teach and hold a view of the Communion called "consubstantiation." This view agrees that science cannot trace the alterations in the elements of bread and wine, but nevertheless such real changes do occur alongside the spiritual presence of Jesus Christ. This spiritual presence of Jesus Christ is quite different from the Roman view and is akin to the Reformed view; the stumbling block is the first part of this faith-statement; namely, that the elements are indeed changed into the real body and blood of our Lord. Thus, Presbyterians do not hold this view either. Presbyterians also open Communion reception to all believers in Christ.

3. A third view is generally held by the Anabaptists and their descendants: the Baptists, many Independents, many of the Campbellites, and Bible churches. This view rejects not only the Roman view and the Lutheran view, but also the Reformed view (to be described momentarily); this view holds that the Eucharist is to be viewed primarily as "an ordinance," a "memorial," an "anniversary," so to speak, of the Last Supper. Its primary purpose is to remind the believer of something that once happened and that Jesus will come

again, as He promised. In some of these congregations this is celebrated something like a family
meal, to which only members of that family may
participate.

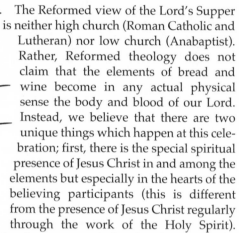

Reformed view of the Lord's Supper

4.   The Reformed view of the Lord's Supper
is neither high church (Roman Catholic and
Lutheran) nor low church (Anabaptist).
Rather, Reformed theology does not
claim that the elements of bread and
wine become in any actual physical
sense the body and blood of our Lord.
Instead, we believe that there are two
unique things which happen at this cele-
bration; first, there is the special spiritual
presence of Jesus Christ in and among the
elements but especially in the hearts of the
believing participants (this is different
from the presence of Jesus Christ regularly
through the work of the Holy Spirit).
Second, we believe that the elements are vital and real reminders of
the brokenness of His body and the loss of His blood for us sinners.
Thus, we see and feel the real presence of Jesus Christ as we partake
and sense the real price of His crucifixion (broken body and shed
blood) as we see, handle, and taste the elements of bread and wine
through which this reality becomes known to us uniquely.

B.   Baptism. There are at least three views of baptism:

1.   There is the view called baptismal regeneration, by which adherents
teach that baptism is God's initiation of persons into His Church in
such a way that the action of baptism so-to-speak almost guarantees
them a place in God's kingdom. This view is taught by the Roman
Catholic Church and held by most Episcopalians and some
Lutherans and Methodists and a few Presbyterians. This view identifies the outward action and timing of baptism with an eternal
relationship with Jesus Christ. Some who experience baptism with
this kind of theology seem to deny the need for any kind of additional personal relationship with Jesus Christ. In other words, in
practice a baptized relationship with the Church takes the place of
any need for a personal relationship with Jesus Christ. Those who
hold these views usually baptize by pouring or sprinkling.

2. A second viewpoint regarding baptism is that called believer's baptism, held by all who count the Anabaptists as their spiritual forebears. This view categorically denies any validity to any baptism of infants or children under the "age of understanding." In this view baptism is reserved only for those who can knowledgeably choose to follow Jesus Christ; this limits candidates to older children, youth, and adults. Hence, it is called believer's baptism. Usually adherents of this view perform all their baptisms in the more dramatic way of immersing candidates, even those who in other traditions had already received baptism by sprinkling or pouring.

3. The third view is held by most Presbyterians and many Lutherans and Methodists. This is called covenant baptism, which may be administered both to believers and to their children, usually by sprinkling or pouring. In this view (the Reformed view) God's family is identified as being composed of "believers and their children." These children are then baptized as infants as an initiation into the family of God; their parents take their faith vows for them and promise to train them in the faith. However, each of these children must, upon reaching the age of understanding, discover what was earlier done for them by their parents; they must be confirmed in that personal faith, making that faith now their own.

Salvation, then, is not tied to the act of baptism; it is tied to the faith of the believer, either a present faith or a future faith, as our God knows the future and is not (like we) tied to the present. Salvation is tied to God's action and God's salvation is not tied to a human action of placing water on one's head. This is true whether we are talking about adults or infants, for salvation is never automatic. We would encourage you to hold this view of baptism.

Presbyterians accept the baptism of all other Christians, if such has been done "with water" and "in the name of the Father, the Son, and the Holy Spirit." Presbyterians hold that baptism

Reformed view of baptism

should only be done once; it is not a repeatable sacrament, while the Lord's Supper should be repeated frequently, especially when there is a need for a personal rededication to Jesus Christ. Presbyterians believe that baptism of children is the New Testament way of including the children of believers, just as in the Old Testament there was the ritual of circumcision, which was used to incorporate the (male) children of believers into the family of God. We are grateful that in the New Testament the way was opened to include the female children of believers into the household of faith. Thus, we see baptism taking the place of circumcision, just as the Eucharist took the place in the New Testament of Passover.

OUTLINE OF CLASS PRESENTATION

Lecture
1. Presbyterian Polity: *The Unique Gift*
2. Ecclesiology Compared
3. Three Basic Forms of Polity
4. Governing Bodies: Map and Charts

Discussion
1. Presbyterian Polity: Questions and Answers
2. Presbyterian Polity Discussion
3. Fitting into Your Church's Church Mission Statement

Examination Instructions

Homework for Session Six
1. Know Session V, pages 93–109.
2. Read Session VI, pages 110–122.
3. Know "Presbyterian Polity: Questions and Answers," pages 103–109.
4. Learn Your Church's "Mission Statement."
5. Catch-up.
6. Try to do at least half of the written exam this week.

Presbyterian Polity:
The Unique Gift
How Presbyterians Govern Themselves

The church word for "governance" or "church government" is "polity," which comes from the same family of words as "politics" and "policy." The way a group of Christians gathered into a church functions and rules themselves says much about their basic theology and influences what they believe and how they live.

Presbyterians put a great deal of effort into their understanding Scripture regarding government and how we interconnect with one another. Presbyterians believe our form of government is biblical, but by this statement we do not hold that all other forms of government are nonbiblical. In fact, as we read Scripture, we also find elements of and suggestions supporting the other two major families of church government.

Presbyterians have sought to build our form of government or polity on seven principles for which we find biblical support:

1. Christ alone is head of the Church; all others are subordinate to Christ. Elected representatives seek first to represent Jesus Christ and only secondarily their constituents;

2. Scripture alone provides Christians with authority and responsibility one for another, but no one form of government is mandated by Scripture for all;

3. All believers equally are to serve as priests for each other; there is no hierarchy of spiritual power except that which honors Christ and upholds the responsibility of every believer for one another;

4. Church power is "joint," not "individual." All church power must be administered "decently and in order" to give God glory;

5. The unity of the Church is best seen as an interconnectedness (connectionalism) through representative assemblies, the larger with oversight over the smaller, rather than through a hierarchy or through mass democratic rule;

6. Under God the people, gathered in congregation, have the right to elect their own leadership, including pastor(s) and church officers; and

7. There must be a parity of ministry among the elected leaders, in our case, this is seen as parity between lay elders and teaching elders (called "Ministers of Word and Sacrament").

Presbyterianism, building upon these above principles, has offered the church and the world a unique gift of representative republican government centered on the lay presbyter (or Ruling Elder), who is not clergy but who exercises similar responsibility for governance as Teaching Elders (Ministers of the Word and Sacrament). These Lay Ruling Elders are ordained, in the same way and with the same responsibility for governance, as the Teaching Elders.

These Lay Ruling Elders, on occasion, may preach and, with specific permission from presbytery on rare occasions and with due need, may administer the Lord's Supper (W-2.4012c). Ordinarily, the administration of the sacraments is the responsibility of a team of elders, which shall include both a Teaching Elder and at least one Ruling Elder.

Decision-making at every level of governing body is a joint venture by both Teaching Elders and Ruling Elders. Every effort is made to require a parity of eldership in all governing bodies above the Session, so that in our annual General Assembly one-half of the voting commissioners are Lay Ruling Elders.

We have discovered in our conversations with those communions represented in COCU that other denominations do not have anything like our office of ordained Lay Ruling Elder and do not know what to make of our unique gift. Other denominations simply do not have the theology nor the ecclesiology that would allow them to trust so much responsibility and power, duty and service to laity; they cannot yet fathom how we Presbyterians can trust laity in such a way and offer ordination to them equal to that of our clergy. This is unthinkable in the hierarchical polity with its "trickle-down" theory of power and responsibility. Among those who adhere to the "bubble-up" theory of the flow of power in the congregational polity, it is illogical to empower selected representatives of the congregation to rule the body and thereby to strip the total congregation of power and responsibility.

Additionally, it is important for all of us to know that when we join a "particular local Presbyterian church congregation," we are also uniting with both our national denomination and the Church Universal. Thus, "membership" is threefold. All who join this particular Presbyterian local church are also joining the Presbyterian Church (U.S.A.); all who trust in Jesus Christ as Savior and Lord also belong to His Church Universal.

Ecclesiology Compared

These three basic forms of polity arise out of three separate sets of presuppositions regarding how God works in and among His people in governance and in revelation and call. Thus, each form of polity is supported by a unique view of ecclesiology; that is, a theology of "the church." Each can best be understood when an analogy is used to describe the group dynamics inherent in the governance system, as noted below in the chart:

WHAT THE CHURCH IS LIKE		
ANABAPTIST VIEW	**PRESBYTERIAN** VIEW	**EPISCOPAL** VIEW
Friends "Voluntary Association"	Family "Connectional"	The Military "Hierarchy"
Baptist/Congregational	Presbyterian/Reformed	Episcopal/Roman Catholic
My Choice	God's Choice ("Put Here by God")	Another's Choice
Duty: "Separate"	Duty: "Reform or Renew"	Duty: "Obey"
Movement: Separatism	Movement: Puritan	Movement: Establishment

THREE BASIC FORMS OF POLITY

There is the **Hierarchical or Episcopal Form,** in which all power flows from top to bottom. (If power were water, this form would best be illustrated by the waterfall.) This theory is that God the Holy Spirit speaks to and gives power to those at the top, who then distribute power in a kind of "trickle-down" theory. There are two major illustrations of this form of government: the monarchical and the oligarchical.

The monarchical subform concentrates power in the leader or single person at the top. In civil government this may be a king or dictator; in religious government we see this form in the Roman Catholic Church with its pope.

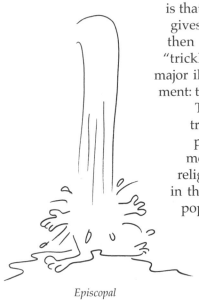

Episcopal

In the oligarchical subform power is found "in the few" at the top. In civil government this could be observed in rule by a council or a court or even by a political party; when it is by three the name might be "a troika"; in religious government this form is best illustrated by the Episcopal Church with its Council of Bishops.

The second kind of government is the **Congregational Form,** which assumes that all power by the Holy Spirit originates at the bottom or among the masses of democracy. (Again if power were water, in this form power would flow like a powerful fountain thrusting gushing water upwards.) Every member theoretically votes on

Congregational

every issue. There are few illustrations of such government functioning for lengthy periods of time in the civil realm, but we do have
historically the Greek city-states and the New England town meetings.
In the religious realm this form of government is the trademark of the
Congregational Church and the Baptist Churches, among others. Over
time there appears to be a tendency for a pure democracy to come
under the authority of some strong indigenous leader who overrules
all the rest.

The Middle Way within polity is the **Presbyterian Form** with its
republican and representative characteristics. In the civil realm we
see this governmental theory in our own United States government;
in the religious arena this form is found in the Reformed and
Presbyterian Churches. This polity lies in between the previously
described two; this is of all polity forms the most complicated.
Within the Presbyterian system we believe the Holy Spirit first gives
power and authority to the people gathered in congregation to elect
their own leadership; the congregation chooses to become affiliated
with the larger Presbyterian body. The congregation elects its elders
and minister(s) who serve as their representatives and form a church
governing body called a "Session" to make all important decisions
for that local church. Presbyterians from all the sessions and
churches within a region form a regional governing body called a
"Presbytery" to make all important decisions for that region.
Presbyterians from all the presbyteries and churches within several
states form both a larger regional governing body called a "Synod"
and with all presbyteries and churches
within the nation form the
national governing body
called the "General
Assembly" (see the map
on the following page).
(Again, if power were
water, the best illustra-
tion for how the
Presbyterian representa-
tive polity works would be an
automated "holy car wash,"
with water [power] coming
from every direction.)

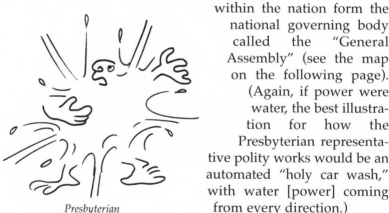

Presbyterian

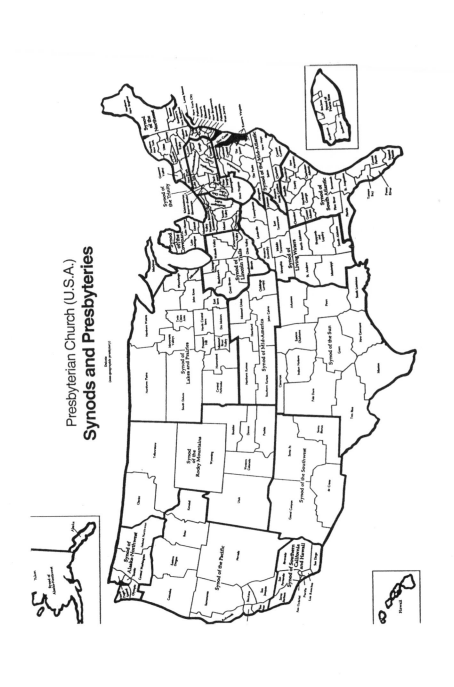

Presbyterian Church (U.S.A.)
Synods and Presbyteries

THE PRESBYTERIAN CHURCH (U.S.A.)
THE GENERAL ASSEMBLY

National—Most Inclusive Governing Body

Meetings:	Annually, rotating in six sections of the nation
Membership:	Each presbytery sends at least one Minister and one Elder. One Minister and one Elder are sent for each additional 10,000 communicants or major fraction thereof.
Officers:	Moderator, elected annually (nonpaid position) Stated Clerk, elected every four years (paid staff)
Communicants:	2,609,191 (as of 12/31/97)
Ministers:	20,858 (as of 12/31/97)
Governing Bodies:	173 presbyteries and 16 synods (as of 12/31/97)
Congregations:	11,295 (as of 12/31/97)
Functions through:	Annual meeting plus General Assembly Council (GAC), Ministry Divisions, Permanent Judicial Commission (PJC), GA Nominating Committee (GANC), GA Committee on Representation (GACOR), GA Advisory Committee on the Constitution (ACC), and others, all of which have paid staff
Responsibilities:	To set priorities in mission for the whole Church; To provide essential program functions to fulfill mission; To administer and serve all approved ministries; To collect funds and supervise their use for their intended missional purposes; To provide communication to/with the whole Church; To create synods and supervise their work; To decide controversies and final adjudication in all judicial disputes and cases; To warn against error in doctrine and immortality in practice; To provide authoritative interpretations; To establish ecumenical relations and to correspond with other churches; To see that less inclusive governing bodies observe the Constitution; To amend the *Book of Order* with concurrence by a simple majority of the presbyteries; and To amend *The Book of Confessions* or to enter into full organic union with another body with concurrence by a two-thirds majority of the presbyteries and a second concurring Assembly.

THE PRESBYTERIAN CHURCH (U.S.A.)
[SAMPLE] THE SYNOD OF THE SUN
(Arkansas-Louisiana-Oklahoma-Texas)

Multistate Governing Body

Meetings: Biennially, with three adjourned meetings

Membership: Each presbytery sends at least one Minister and one Elder with additional commissioners according to presbytery size and an agreed-upon formula

Officers: Moderator, elected biennially (nonpaid position)
Stated Clerk, elected every four years (part-time paid staff)

Communicants: 213,962 (as of 12/31/97)

Ministers: 1,550 (as of 12/31/97)

Governing Bodies: 11 presbyteries (as of 12/31/97)

Congregations: 948 (as of 12/31/97)

Functions through: Semiannual meetings of the Synod Assembly plus Synod Permanent Judicial Commission, Synod Nominating Committee, Synod Committee on Representation, and other service agencies

Responsibilities: To set priorities in mission for its four-state region;
To coordinate with Assembly and presbyteries for all church work in its four-state region;
To administer and serve all approved ministries;
To provide communication to/with all its constituencies;
To create presbyteries and to consult with them in their mission and work;
To provide resources for presbyteries with less resources;
To collect funds and to supervise their use for their intended purposes;
To coordinate the work of presbyteries in relation to their ministers;
To serve in judicial matters in accordance with the Constitution and to adjudicate cases arising within synod;
To warn against error in doctrine and immorality in practice within its region;
To review the records of the constituent presbyteries to assure conformity to the Constitution;
To superintend the work of all regional service agencies and educational institutions under its care; and
To establish regional ecumenical relationships.

THE PRESBYTERIAN CHURCH (U.S.A.)
[SAMPLE] GRACE PRESBYTERY
(North Central and Northeast Texas)

Regional Governing Body

Meetings:	Quarterly
Membership:	All Ministers working and living in area plus at least one Elder from each Session, with at least one Elder for each Minister on a church's staff plus other Elders to bring parity between Ministers and Elders
Officers:	Moderator, elected annually (nonpaid position)
	Stated Clerk, elected by term (paid position)
Communicants:	50,941 (as of 12/31/97)
Ministers:	341 (as of 12/31/97)
Governing Bodies:	185 organized churches (as of 12/31/97)
Functions through:	Quarterly meetings plus Presbytery Council, Presbytery Committee on Ministry, Presbytery Nominations Committee, Presbytery Committee on Representation, Presbytery Permanent Judicial Commission, and other divisions, committees, and agencies
Responsibilities:	To set priorities in mission for its area;
	To elect commissioners to General Assembly and Synod;
	To provide encouragement, guidance, resources, and coordination to its member churches in their ministries;
	To provide pastoral care for its churches and ministers, visiting sessions and ministers often;
	To organize new churches and to divide, dismiss, or dissolve churches in consultation with their members;
	To control the location of new and relocating churches;
	To take oversight of churches without pastors;
	To support and direct those who would be Candidates for the Ministry;
	To ordain, install, dismiss, remove, and discipline Ministers;
	To collect funds for mission and to see that they are spend for their intended purposes;
	To create, support, and supervise mission service agencies;
	To serve in judicial matters arising within presbytery;
	To assume original jurisdiction of a church, when necessary;
	To review all sessional minutes; and
	To approve appropriate congregational property alterations.

PRESBYTERIAN POLITY: QUESTIONS AND ANSWERS

1. **Who is the Head of the Presbyterian Church (U.S.A.)?**
   Jesus Christ is the only Head and King of His Church.

2. **What are "the Great Ends of the Church"?**
   The Great Ends of the Church are:
   a. the proclamation of the gospel for the salvation of humankind;
   b. the shelter, nurture, and spiritual fellowship of the children of God;
   c. the maintenance of divine worship;
   d. the preservation of the truth;
   e. the promotion of social righteousness; and
   f. the exhibition of the Kingdom of Heaven to the world.

3. **Is a church officer's first loyalty to the people who elected him/her?**
   No, it is first to the Head of the Church, Jesus Christ.

4. **What are the three basic forms of church government and list two denominations which use each form.**
   They are the Episcopal, the Congregational, and the Presbyterian forms of government.
   Episcopal—Roman Catholic Church, Methodist Church
   Congregational—Church of Christ, Baptist Church
   Presbyterian—Reformed Church, Presbyterian Church

5. **Illustrate each of these three basic forms of government in the civic realm.**
   Episcopal—a monarchy or an oligarchy
   Congregational—New England town meeting or Greek city-state
   Presbyterian—United States of America (a republic)

6. **What forms the Constitution of the Presbyterian Church (U.S.A.)?**
   The Constitution of the Presbyterian Church (U.S.A.) includes *The Book of Confessions* with its eleven confessional documents and the *Book of Order* with its three parts: "Form of Government," "Directory for Worship," and "Rules of Discipline."

7. **Presbyterian Church Government is organized in a series of graded *governing bodies*. Name them in order.**
   Session, Presbytery, Synod, and General Assembly.

8. **What are the titles of the three ordained offices in the Presbyterian Church (U.S.A.)?**
   Ministers (of Word and Sacrament) and Elders (both of whom are also known as "Presbyters") and Deacons

9. **Compare the qualifications for these three offices.**
   Generally, the qualifications for all three are similar and very high. Candidates for any and all of these offices should be sound in the faith, blameless in life, spiritual in character, an example of Christian conduct. The particular emphasis laid down for the Minister is a competency of human learning as well as theological training; for the Elder, wisdom and discretion and an aptness to teach; for the Deacon, warm sympathies and a concern for those in need.

10. **What are the powers reserved for the congregation?**
    The congregation has the right to elect its own Pastor(s), Elders, and Deacons and to be consulted concerning matters of special importance affecting the property of the church.

11. **Name and define the kind of power church officers exercise.**
    Church officers, not as individuals but as they sit in governing bodies, exercise joint power which is entirely ecclesiastical in nature, never civil.

12. **What is the proper title now given to anyone who presides over any section of the Presbyterian government: a task force, a subcommittee, a committee, a commission, a board, or a governing body?**
    Moderator

13. **What is the difference in Presbyterian polity between a committee and a commission?**
    A committee functions for and reports back to its appointing body with suggestions called recommendations; a commission is authorized to act for its appointing body and reports back its actions as accomplished facts.

14. **How is a local congregation, called a particular church, related to the total Presbyterian body?**
    The Session which rules the particular church, under the Presbyterian Constitution, elects commissioners to the next higher governing body, the presbytery.

15. **What are the essential three parts of a "call" to service to God as a church officer?**

    a. the inward testimony of a good conscience on the part of the person;

    b. the manifest approbation of God's people on the part of the church; and

    c. the concurring judgment of a lawful governing body of the church.

16. **Should there be a difference of opinion between the Session and the Board of Deacons (Diaconate), who in Presbyterian order has the right to overrule whom?**

    Although Deacons and Elders equally are called by God based upon the same general spiritual qualifications, in the Presbyterian system the Session rules all aspects of the particular church, including the Board of Deacons.

17. **What is one's duty if he/she should find himself/herself totally out of accord with an action of the governing body of which he/she is a part?**

    "When a matter is determined (constitutionally) by a majority vote, every member shall either actively concur with or passively submit to such determination; or if his conscience permits him to do neither, he shall, after sufficient liberty modestly to reason and remonstrate, peaceably withdraw from our communion without attempting to make any schism."*

18. **Ordination, we are told, is for life, but active service comes in limited terms. Explain what is expected of the "Reserve" Elder or Deacon.**

    "Reserve" Elders and Deacons are expected to continue throughout their lives in their respective ministries and callings, as they are able, though only during their active terms shall they participate in the governance of the Session or the decision-making of the Diaconate. Otherwise, there are many particular aspects of their calling which they can accomplish as alert and continuing officers of the church.

19. **Who is constitutionally charged with the responsibility of building the annual church budget? What part must the congregation play?**

    The Session shall build the budget, though wise Sessions find ways to incorporate the thinking of the Deacons and of the congregation-at-large in some manner prior to the Session's formal adoption of the church budget. Any and all changes in compensation to any minister must gain the approval of the congregation and presbytery.

---

* Footnote to G-6.0107b, PC(USA) *Book of Order.*

20. **How should Presbyterians respond to the pronouncements of higher governing bodies?**

With interest and appreciation, with seriousness and a willingness to test all such by the Scripture, the *Confessions*, and human conscience, ever remembering that such bodies do not speak for God, nor for all Presbyterians, nor for the Presbyterian Church, except as it is representatively gathered. We must take such statements seriously, fully aware that such are but the majority opinion of that group of presbyters gathered at that moment in time. We are fully aware that all church governing bodies err; we are always aware that we err. We must hear and take heed to the valid aspects of their spiritual wisdom, keeping their statements in perspective.

PRESBYTERIAN POLITY DISCUSSION: AN OVERVIEW OF THE *BOOK OF ORDER*

A review of the PC(USA) *Book of Order* through its table of contents reveals that the first four chapters deal with foundational matters: preliminary principles (which declare our view of the One who is the Head of the Church, the six great ends or purposes of the Church, along with our historic principles of church order and government and a definition of our Constitution), our view of the value and use of our confessions, and a discussion of our understanding of the mission and unity of the Church. On the other hand, the last four chapters describe our ecumenical commitment, how we form union churches or governing bodies, and how we amend our Constitution.

From the beginning it is clear that Presbyterians are people of the books: the Bible, *The Book of Confessions* (which describes our theology), and lastly the *Book of Order* (which describes our polity). Our ordination vows inform us that these three books go from highest authority to least authority, yet all are authoritative for all Presbyterian ordinands. A study of the early chapters of the *Book of Order* enables us to understand that we have a long history rooted both in radical (foundational) governmental concepts as well as historic agreements which define us. The noted six "great ends of the Church" provide for us a definition of what the Church should be about; each congregation and each officer should examine themselves to see how we fit into this set of purposes. In the second chapter we come to understand that Presbyterians are reformers—past, present, and future— that is, the job of renewing the church, having once been done, must always continue to be our task. The Church must always be recalled to its scriptural roots. We must ever seek to reflect biblical truth in both faith and practice; this is accomplished by the work of the Holy Spirit and by constant returning to Scripture for God's Word in every circumstance. "Reformed, always being reformed, by the Holy Spirit, according to the Word of God" must not only be our motto but our way of life. Many have noted the lyric quality of the third chapter in its challenge to faithfulness in mission. In chapter four we seek to clarify our understanding of God's expectations of the church's inclusivity and unity.

The core of the *Book of Order* is found in chapters five through fourteen, where we find detail about our biblical understanding of church membership and church officership, as well as how we view a local or "particular" church (congregation) and its property. Great detail describes our four governing bodies in general and then in specifics: the session, the presbytery, the synod, and the General Assembly. A full understanding of these matters will set us apart as a people of God clearly "Presbyterian," as over against those Christians who see things from an hierarchical or congregational perspective. We are not better than they, but our understandings of how best to reflect biblical truth for the church operation is uniquely different. Presbyterian polity works wondrously well when properly implemented; yet, we sinners can take this good and effective government and "gum up the works" severely. It should be the purpose of every Presbyterian ordinand to understand how we best function and to implement that understanding, with a double portion of grace, lest we become legalists and slaves to a law.

The two most important chapters for new Presbyterian ordinands to understand in their preordination training are chapters six and fourteen. Former General Assembly Stated Clerk Jim Andrews had it right when he said:

Representative government depends upon carefully chosen officers convened in the presence of Jesus Christ to carry out the mission of the Church. As long as one maintains that focus of devotion, that pattern of shared ministry, [ordinands] will be following the government of our polity and abiding by the discipline of our denomination.

What do you think the phrases "convened in the presence of Jesus Christ" and "that pattern of shared ministry" mean? Are all elders, including our minister elders, to sense ownership for what transpires not only in our sessions, but also in our presbyteries, our synods, and our General Assembly?

In practice the session's faith, view of mission, brotherly/sisterly practice, and level of responsibility-bearing for the life of their particular or local church determines whether our congregation grows or dies, is faithful or faithless, is filled with strife or peace, holds a worldview or is hopelessly provincial. In a real sense and on a human level, each session has the power of life or death in its hands for its congregation. This challenge is so great that it can be successfully fulfilled only by the power of a Living God indwelling each session member. The same may be said of the presbytery, that key governing body, that can bring life or death to the particular churches and ministers under its care and authority. To Presbyterians the life and witness of sessions and presbyteries make the difference for their constituents in our obedience to our Lord and enjoyment of the Christian life of worship and service, evangelism and outreach, mission and witness to which we all are called.

A thorough study of chapter fourteen should lead each once again to self-inspection and a deep spiritual review of our lives, as we prepare to take our ordination/installation vows. We officers are through ordination "set apart" uniquely to do God's work in our assigned vineyard; it is incumbent upon us to be spiritually mature, morally fit, biblically knowledgeable, and thoroughly trained to accomplish the enormous challenges being set before us. Only by working collegially and only in Christ can we do it!

Our Church's Mission Statement

The Mission
of
(First) Presbyterian Church, Anywhere, U.S.A.
is

_____

_____

_____

_____

_____

_____

_____

_____

_____

_____

_____

A Word to the Leader

At this point please provide each of your officers-elect with a copy of your church's mission statement, either as a handout or as a copy to be pasted into this textbook, above. If you should not yet have a mission statement, you may wish, as a teaching tool, to consider the value of the one used at my local church, as noted below:

The Mission of Highland Park Presbyterian Church of Dallas is
to glorify God and enjoy Him by:

Worshiping
Proclaiming and spreading the good news of God's saving grace in Jesus Christ
Nurturing the congregation through education, fellowship, and compassion
Ministering to the community and the world in the name of Jesus Christ and
through
the power of the Holy Spirit
Being a responsible member of the Presbyterian Church (U.S.A.)

OUTLINE OF CLASS PRESENTATION

ELDERS

Lecture
1. Elders in the Bible and the *Book of Order*
2. Duties of the Session
3. Sample Organization for a Session
4. Sample Agenda—Session Meeting

Discussion
>
> Guidelines—Practical Suggestions
> Session's Local Church Ministry
> Functional Data

DEACONS

Lecture—Using a Question and Answer Format
1. Biblical Teaching about Deacons
2. The *Book of Order* and the Deacon
3. Duties of the Diaconate (UPCUSA Heritage)
4. Duties of the Diaconate (PCUS Heritage)

Discussion
>
> Guidelines—Practical Suggestions
> Diaconate's Local Church Ministry
> Functional Data

Homework for This Week
1. Know Session VI, pages 110–122.
2. Finish Written Examination and Turn in to Committee.
3. Study for Oral Examination.

ELDERS IN THE BIBLE
AND THE *BOOK OF ORDER*

This study leads us to turn within the *Book of Order* to G-6.0300 for the description of the nature of the office of Elder, the Scriptural practice, his/her governmental responsibilities, his/her gifts and requirements, and a listing of specific responsibilities.

This study continues as we turn to G-10.000 for our Constitution's description of the Session in Presbyterian governance. The new officer should especially focus on the listing of the responsibilities of the Session, what is said about the Session's Moderator and meetings, Minutes and records, and church finances. Observe what is said about the Session's duties when the church is without an installed pastor.

Take time now to read and study particularly G-6.0300 and G-10.0102.

Let us now study the Scriptures about the office of Elder:

A. Biblical basis
    Exodus 18:21–26
    Luke 22:24–26

B. As outlined in the *Book of Order* (G-6.0300-6.0304)

C. Biblical References regarding qualifications and duties:
    1. 1 Timothy 3:1–7
    2. 1 Timothy 4:14–16
    3. 2 Timothy 1:6–9
    4. 2 Timothy 2:1–3
    5. 1 Timothy 5:17
    6. 2 Timothy 4:2–5
    7. Acts 4:1–2
    8. Titus 1:10–11
    9. Titus 1:6–9
    10. 1 Peter 5:1–4
    11. Hebrews 13:7, 9, 17–18

DUTIES OF THE SESSION

An outline of the responsibilities of the Session might enable elders to grasp the scope of their duties and to think creatively about their own life and the ministry to which they have been called, elected, and ordained. It is suggested that readers who serve on sessions study carefully chapter X in the *Book of Order* and work through the following outline with care. Responsibilities and powers of the Session for the mission and oversight of a particular church include the following:

A. As a whole:
    1. Training, examining, ordaining, and installing all church officers (Elders and Deacons) and ensuring that all are assigned particular duties in line with their gifts and interests as well as supervising and being responsible for all individual Elders and all subunits of the Session and all other units of ministry, mission, and fellowship within the congregation.
    2. Supervising the maintenance of all church rolls and encouraging all members to fulfill their membership obligations.
    3. Calling all necessary congregational meetings and fulfilling all lawful expectations of higher governing bodies.
    4. Fulfilling all *Book of Order* requirements relating to judicial matters.
    5. Supervising all the other work of God within that particular church, as it may be assigned to specific Committees/Councils of the Session and to the Board of Deacons (unless that church has opted not to have such).

B. The work of a Benevolences/Mission Committee:
    1. Review of all benevolence/mission requests, evaluating and determining what shall be underwritten and by how much, including all requests for mission support from higher governing bodies.

C. The work of a Christian Education/Nurture Committee:
    1. Developing and supervising the total churchwide educational program.
    2. Supervising all scout programs, all schools the church may sponsor, all recreational programs, all special age-appropriate ministries.
    3. Developing and supervising all ministries of congregational care, often in partnership with the minister(s).

D. The work of a Denominational Affairs/Church Courts Committee:
    1. Encouraging and supporting, as well as ministering to and with all higher governing bodies, including education of the Session on all issues of import within the church and community.

2. Selecting qualified persons to serve as Commissioners to higher governing bodies and to serve on the structures of such entities in approved inclusive ways.

3. Seeking to carry out all lawful instructions from other governing bodies and petitioning them through overtures on matters of import to the Session.

4. Involving the Session in the ecumenical church and in approved community activities and joint witness opportunities.

E. The work of an Evangelism/Outreach Committee:
   1. Leading the congregation in reaching out in mission and witness both to the local community and to the whole world.
   2. Seeking to win all to Christ through intentional methods of evangelism and meeting human needs through outreach and compassion.
   3. Encouraging through faithfulness to Scripture the renewal and reformation of the particular church and all its members to a more vital and dynamic personal faith with community ramifications.
   4. Enlisting both youth and adult new members through faithful and intentional efforts of evangelism through confirmation and inquirers classes and new member education.
   5. Enlisting church members for ministry and professional service within the church.

F. The work of a Personnel Committee:
   1. Assisting the particular church to find and fairly compensate and supervise personnel to meet all its staffing needs, working with the presbytery and the congregation in the calling of ordained staff.

G. The work of a Program Planning/Budgeting Committee:
   1. Providing a means for the evaluation of proposed new programs and the elimination of outworn old programs.
   2. Development of an annual budget for Sessional approval and congregational education.

H. The work of a Stewardship Committee:
   1. Challenging the congregation with the opportunity of responsible stewardship of time, talents, and treasure.
   2. Providing structure to the recruitment, training, and placement of volunteers in the work of ministry within and through that particular church for the Kingdom.

I. The work of a Worship/Work Committee:
   1. With the Minister(s) providing for the worship of God's people, the hearing of the preached Word, the administration of the Sacraments,

　　and the supervision of the music program.
　2. Supervising specific supplemental needs of the worshiping community through fellowship, ushering, greeting, radio/television outreach, etc.

J.　The work of the Diaconate:
　1. Oversight of the distribution of the gifts of the church, the ministries to the unemployed or needy, and the daily supervision of business practices policies.
　2. Oversight of all church-owned properties, including investments.

SAMPLE ORGANIZATION FOR A SESSION

The session is responsible for planning, organizing, directing, and implementing all efforts at our particular church to fulfill our church's "Statement of Mission" and the PC(U.S.A.)'s "Great Ends of the Church." All spiritual authority and responsibility for this local mission resides in the Session, aided and abetted by the church's called and employed staff. To meet these goals this sample session has chosen to organize itself into eight major Committees or Councils, each with (sub)committees as needed, as follows:

I.　**Benevolence (Mission) Council**
　　Prepares the Benevolence (Mission) budget, monitors contributions, and provides direction to the church of its benevolence program.
　　Budget Committee
　　Evaluation Committee

II.　**Christian Education Council**
　　Is responsible for developing and maintaining the total educational work of this church.
　　Adult Education Committee
　　　Bethel Bible Training Subcommittee
　　　Ministry Institute Subcommittee
　　Children's Committee
　　　Child Care Subcommittee
　　　Early Childhood Subcommittee
　　　Elementary Education Subcommittee
　　Curriculum Committee
　　Day School Committee
　　Library Committee

Scouting Committee
Singles Committee
Space Allocation Committee
University Ministry Committee
Youth Committee

III. **Church Courts (Denominational Affairs) Council**
Is responsible for the relationships between this particular church
and the denomination with which we are an integral part and
for all local ministries directed towards our governing bodies
or within the PC(U.S.A.), including a seminary intern program.
Congregational Concerns Committee
General Assembly Concerns Committee
Presbytery Concerns Committee
Public Affairs Committee

IV. **Evangelism and Outreach Council**
Is responsible for planning and implementing the witness of this
particular church in the world, both at home and abroad.
Evangelism Committee
List Enlistment Committee
New Member Committee
Celebrations and Follow-through Subcommittee
Leadership Subcommittee
New Member Class Subcommittee
Preparations and Prospects Subcommittee
TV Outreach Committee
Urban/USA Missions Committee
World Missions Committee
Vacation-with-a-Purpose Subcommittee
World Outreach Weekend Subcommittee
World Relief and Hunger Committee

V. **Personnel Council**
Formulates policies and procedures regarding administrative and
personnel management of the church and identifies future
leadership.
Compensation and Benefits Committee
Job Description, Evaluation, and Review Committee
Search and Interview Committee

VI. **Program Planning and Budget Council**
Recommends and implements long-range plans, acts in advisory
capacity to the Session, oversees the preparation of the church

budget, and evaluates progress in implementation of plans and application of policies.

Long-range Planning Committee

VII. Stewardship Council

Encourages and educates the congregation in their desire to be good stewards of time, abilities, and possessions, and is in charge of the annual fall stewardship campaign to underwrite the church budget.

VIII. Worship and Work Council

Assists the minister(s) and the Session in interpreting to the congregation in the meaning and experience of worship.

Fellowship Time Committee

Greeters Committee

Music Committee

Prayer Support Committee

    Subcommittee for United Prayer in the Sanctuary

    Moms in Prayer Subcommittee

    Prayer Room Ministry Subcommittee

Radio/Television Ministry Committee

Sacraments Committee

Ushers Committee

Worship Committee

GUIDELINES—PRACTICAL SUGGESTIONS
SESSION'S LOCAL CHURCH HISTORY
FUNCTIONAL DATA

A Word to the Leader

After teaching the above material on the session with the elders-elect, it is important to focus on how your local church session has divided itself to do its work, according to your needs and understanding. Therefore, after teaching the biblical basis of the office, the constitutional warrant for this office, and the responsibilities of the session, you should lead your elders-elect quickly through the above sample sessional organization and sample sessional agenda to focus most of your time on how you do the work of the session locally. Specifically, your candidates for office will want to know your time commitment expectations, the schedule of your meetings, the duties of each committee on which they may serve, along with such questions as: how do we now do things, how do we change things when change is needed, how do we develop the budget, etc.

Use your time wisely to inform these new leaders of how they may best fit in with your current methods and procedures to accomplish God's work on the session of your church.

One sample training course for elders at this point dealt with the following practical matters:

1. Session Meeting Schedule and Attendance Expectations
2. Elder Committee Assignments and Duty Expectations
3. Guidelines for Elder Assistance at Baptisms
4. Guidelines for Elder Participation in the Services of Holy Communion (with a practice run)
5. Elder Responsibility in Teaching in the Youth Confirmation Program
6. Elder Congregational Visitation Expectations and Home Communion Expectations
7. Elder Involvement in Occasional Services of Communion and Prayer for Wholeness and Healing Services

SAMPLE AGENDA—SESSION MEETING DATE

1. Opening Prayer

2. Clerk's Business
   a. Approve Minutes of [date] meeting
   b. Excuses for absence
   c. Communications
   d. Coordinating Committee Report

3. Diaconate Minutes of [date] meeting

4. Presbyterian Women Report—President

5. Membership Report

6. Council Reports:
   a. Benevolence—Moderator
   b. Christian Education—Moderator
   c. Church Courts—Moderator
   d. Evangelism and Outreach—Moderator
   e. Personnel—Moderator
   f. Program Planning and Budget—Moderator
   g. Stewardship—Moderator
   h. Worship and Work—Moderator

7. Old Business:

8. New Business:

9. Next Stated Meeting—[date]

10. Adjournment with Prayer

DEACONS IN THE BIBLE AND THE *BOOK OF ORDER:* QUESTIONS AND ANSWERS

1. **Where do we find a biblical basis for establishing the office of Deacon?**

   When the Church was just beginning its new life (after Pentecost in Jerusalem), the office was begun in the selection of the seven to take care of certain duties so as to free the apostles for their preaching of the Word. (See Acts 6:1–6)

2. **Is there other evidence that there were Deacons in the Early Church?**

   The word itself appears in a number of places and specific instructions about the qualifications for deacons are given in 1 Timothy, Titus, and 1 Peter.

3. **What is the underlying idea in the role of the Deacon?**

   The word itself (from a Greek word, *diakoneo*) carries the idea of service. The role of servant is a noble one, since our Lord Himself gives us the supreme example of One who came to serve.

4. **How is the idea expressed in the description of the Deacon in the *Book of Order* of the Presbyterian Church (U.S.A.)?**

   G-6.0401 says: "The office of Deacon as set forth in Scripture is one of sympathy, witness, and service after the example of Jesus Christ."

5. **How does the *Book of Order* sum up the characteristics of a Deacon?**

   G-6.0401 goes on to say: "Persons of spiritual character, honest repute, exemplary lives, brotherly and sisterly love, warm sympathies, and sound judgment should be chosen for this office."

6. **How is a group of Deacons to be organized in a local church?**

   The Deacons as elected by the congregation are organized into a "board," and the Board has its own Moderator, selected from among its members. A secretary keep the records of the Board's proceedings.

7. **What is the relationship of the Board of Deacons (Diaconate) to the Session?**

   As in all Presbyterian churches, the entire life of the church is the responsibility of and under the jurisdiction of the Session. The Board of Deacons is therefore under the Session's authority, which relationship is exercised in a formal sense by the Session's review of the Minutes of the Board's meetings. In many congregations, a closeness between the two groups is fostered by the fact that some regular meetings include a joint meeting of both the Session and the Diaconate (for supper, fellowship, and certain presentations).

8. **How may Deacons best fulfill the high privilege and responsibility of this office?**

They can first of all seek to grow in their own spiritual walk so as to be the kind of disciple of the Lord Jesus Christ described in the scriptural passages as the "ideal deacon." They can encourage others, by word and example, to join them in that kind of growth. They can be faithful in their attendance and participation in meetings and activities which are a part of their deacon's role and seek other avenues of living out their call to service as these become available to them.

9. **What are some practical means by which a Deacon can use to help personal spiritual growth?**

The "means of grace" are available to us for this goal, most especially the Word, the sacraments, and prayer.

10. **Why is it that Diaconates widely differ in their duties and assignments?**

Our denomination, the Presbyterian Church (U.S.A.), was formed in 1983 from the former UPCUSA ("Northern Church") and the former PCUS ("Southern Church"). These two developed over time very different understandings and usages of their Diaconates. However, the "Plan of Union," which brought about the formation of the PC(U.S.A.), included both views of the Diaconate; therefore, either is constitutional and acceptable and may be found effectively working in numerous churches.

11. **What is the "Northern" understanding of the Diaconate?**

The UPCUSA retained as the primary, and often the only, duty of the Diaconate the ministry of sympathy and service. Thus, in many churches following this model the Diaconate functions very much as a committee of ministry to the poor, the sick, the homeless, and/or as a committee providing care for the congregation and the community. Those churches choosing this form for the Diaconate often also organize a "Board of Trustees" to function for the congregation in financial matters; such as, receiving and disbursing church funds, oversight of church endowments and investments, and care for the church's property. Effectively, those with these inclinations often function with a Session (for spiritual matters), a Diaconate (for compassion matters), and a Board of Trustees (for financial matters). Constitutionally, this works only if both the Diaconate and the Board of Trustees are willing to submit to the spiritual authority of the Session.

12. **What is the "Southern" understanding of the Diaconate?**
    The pattern in the PCUS was for the Diaconate to function both as a body for sympathy and service, compassion and care for both congregation and community, as well as the structure responsible, under the Session's direction, in all matters of property care, some matters of financial oversight (including receiving and disbursing church funds and supervision of church business practices), and often ushering and general assistance to the Session. In this system, the Session usually retained oversight of any church endowments and investments and initiatives for major property changes (buying and selling of real estate, with the concurrence of the congregation). In the PCUS Trustees were not normally organized into any separate "board" and always served as "signatories" only for the congregation and/or Session in any civil legal matters requiring such. Thus, the office of Trustee was minor in the PCUS and major in the UPCUSA.

13. **Some churches do not have a Board of Deacons. Is this permissible? How is "Deacons' work" done in such situations?**
    Constitutionally it is permissible for a congregation to determine that it will function without a Board of Deacons. In such cases, the work normally done by the Diaconate is to be done by the Session.

Sample Organization for a Board of Deacons (Southern Background)

Through the committees related to congregational care, this Diaconate carries primary responsibility for proper care to this local church's membership. This effectively means that every deacon serves on some committee or subcommittee of congregational care ministries.

In addition to the ministries below, the pastor(s) provide: individual pastoral care at the time of death or illness; grief; job and financial stresses; guidance for individual and family relationship issues, including marital conflict and divorce; support and referral for drug, alcohol, and mental heath issues; intercessory prayer; support and skills development for members in ministry; preparation for marriage; preparation for baptism; and other ministries tailored to meet parishioner needs.

Congregational Care Ministries
    Senior Adult Ministries
    Pastoral Care Ministries
        Care Connection
        Grief Care
        Divorce Recovery
    Practical Concern Ministries
        Congregational Care Fund
        Career Transition/Job Search
Christian Service and Leadership (Volunteer) Development
Family Life Counseling Center
Business Practices and Administration Committee
Finance Committee
New Member Committee
Print Communications Committee
Property Committee
Ushering Committee

GUIDELINES—PRACTICAL SUGGESTIONS
DIACONATE'S LOCAL CHURCH MINISTRY
FUNCTIONAL DATA

A Word to the Leader

After teaching the above material in the class with the deacons-elect, it is important to focus on how your local diaconate has divided itself to do its work, according to your needs and understanding. Therefore, after teaching the biblical basis of the office, the constitutional warrant for this office, and the responsibilities of the diaconate, you should lead your deacons-elect quickly through the above sample diaconate organization, if it fits, to focus most of your time on how you do the work of the diaconate locally. Specifically, your candidates for office will want to know your time commitment expectations, the schedule of your meetings, the duties of each committee on which they may serve, along with such questions as: how do we now do things, how do we change things when change is needed, how do we fulfill our assigned ministries, etc.

Use your time wisely to inform these new leaders of how they may best fit in with your current methods and procedures to accomplish God's work on the diaconate of your church.

HOW TO PREPARE FOR ORAL EXAMINATION

1. Bathe your preparation time in prayer.
2. Recommit yourself to the Lord.
3. Review the Constitution: *The Book of Confessions* and the *Book of Order*.
4. Study again the Lists of "Questions and Answers:"
   Presbyterian Doctrine
   Presbyterian Discipline
   Presbyterian Polity
   The Duties of the Office to which you have been called
5. Come to the examination with confidence, confidence in the Lord.

What to Expect
1. Circles of three officers-elect plus one elder and one minister (who will examine the officers-elect)
2. Friendly faces and supportive fellow officers praying for you

Purpose
Not to fail nor to embarrass you, but to give you an opportunity to share what you have learned in a positive, affirming setting with your fellow new officers.

ORAL EXAMINATION
[DAY, DATE, LOCATION, TIME]

Schedule for Oral Examination of New Candidates for Office
Please report to [location].
Instructions: Begin on time at _____. Begin with prayer in each group.
Suggested Time-Use Guidelines: For Each Candidate

30 minutes	At least one question, arising out of his/her written statement of Christian Experience
35 minutes	At least two questions on Doctrine and Sacraments
20 minutes	At least two questions on Polity
10 minutes	At least one question on Discipline
15 minutes	At least two questions on Duties of his/her Office
10 minutes	Oral Evaluation of Course and Closing Prayer

Written exams are due at [location] on [day, date, time]
Ordination/Installation [day, date, time] Session Meeting
[Day, date, time] Worship Service

SAMPLE WRITTEN EXAM   NAME: _____

New Church Officers
(First) Presbyterian Church, Anywhere, U.S.A.

First Six Questions Are Required
Please answer two more questions from six optional questions.

Due no later than [Time—Day—Date]
(We urge you to turn in your exam in the week prior to that day.)

QUESTION 1: REQUIRED

My Testimony of My Christian Experience
  (Please include in your salvation story the name of at least one person and two Bible verses God used by the Holy Spirit to bring you to Christ.)
  In lieu of rewriting your "testimony," please attach your three-page written statement to this page, noting the above instruction to be sure that you include these expectations.

_____

_____

_____

_____

_____

_____

_____

_____

_____

_____

_____

QUESTION 2: REQUIRED

Doctrine and Ethos

I. Please list the "Essential Tenets of the Reformed Faith," as noted in the
Book of Order, Chapter 2, as discussed in Session III.

    A. Those we hold in common with the Church Catholic:
        1. _____
        2. _____

    B. Those we hold in common with all heirs of the Protestant Reformation:
        3. _____
        4. _____

    C. Those which are expressly characteristics of the Reformed Tradition:
        5. _____
        6. _____
        7. _____
        8. _____
        9. _____
      10. _____

II. List three likenesses and three differences between the Presbyterian
Church and the Episcopal and/or Lutheran churches (both of which are
strong Christian churches and allies in the Christian family):

Likenesses:
    1. _____
    2. _____
    3. _____

Differences:
    1. _____
    2. _____
    3. _____

III. List three likenesses and three differences between the Presbyterian
Church and the Baptist Churches (which also are strong Christian
Churches and allies in the Christian family):

Likenesses:
    1. _____
    2. _____
    3. _____

Differences:

    1. _____

    2. _____

    3. _____

IV. Contrast "the three waves" of the Reformation in respect to how they differed from the Roman Catholic "norm" of that day and how they differed from each other:

"Modest Reformation" _____

_____

_____

_____

_____

_____

"Thoroughgoing Reformation" _____

_____

_____

_____

_____

_____

"Radical Reformation" _____

_____

_____

_____

_____

_____

"Roman Catholic Counter-Reformation" _____

_____

_____

_____

_____

_____

QUESTION 3: REQUIRED

Doctrine

The motto of the Presbyterian Church (U.S.A.) is *ecclesia reformata, semper reformanda* (G-2.0200).

There is a right way and a wrong way to interpret this affirmation. How we interpret this theological principle determines, to a large measure, our view towards God, God's self-revelation, Scripture, and the nature of faith.

A. What is the right way to interpret this claim and what values are maintained with this view?

_____
_____
_____
_____
_____
_____
_____
_____
_____

B. What is the wrong way to interpret this claim and to what dangers does this lead?

_____
_____
_____
_____
_____
_____
_____
_____
_____

QUESTION 4: REQUIRED

Sacraments

A. The Lord's Supper

Identify and describe four different views of this Sacrament and list the values and problems *(from the Reformed perspective)* of the view italicized:

View 1 (Roman Catholic): _____

_____

Values: _____

_____

Problems: _____

_____

View 2 (Lutheran): _____

View 3 (Reformed): _____

View 4 (Anabaptist): _____

B. Baptism

Identify three different views of Baptism (check [X] the "Reformed View")

View 1: _____

View 2: _____

View 3: _____

Discuss the relationship between baptism and salvation, from a "Reformed" perspective:

_____
_____
_____
_____
_____
_____
_____
_____
_____

QUESTION 5: REQUIRED

Church Polity

A. Presbyterianism offers the whole Church "a unique gift" of governance by ordained _____ who share power with Teaching Elders (Ministers of Word and Sacrament).

B. Describe the values in this form of government and this unique gift and how this polity differs from the other two major forms of government.

_____

_____

_____

C. "True" or "False"—Please answer each:

____ 1. Associate Pastors are not entitled to vote at Session meetings.

____ 2. Confessing members of other Christian churches may present children for baptism.

____ 3. The Pastor(s) shall have sole responsibility for preparing those who would become members of the congregation.

____ 4. Each church shall elect a Board of Deacons.

____ 5. The minutes and records kept by each Session shall be reviewed annually by the presbytery.

____ 6. The Pastor shall be a member of the Church Nominating Committee, serving ex-officio and without vote.

____ 7. An inactive member of a congregation is entitled to all the rights and privileges of an active member except the right to speak in the congregational meetings and to vote and hold office.

____ 8. The Board of Deacons shall develop the Annual Church Budget and obtain approval from the congregation.

____ 9. To do regular business a Session needs a quorum of more than half its Elder members plus its Pastor Moderator.

____ 10. The Session has original jurisdiction in a disciplinary case involving a pastor of the church.

QUESTION 6: REQUIRED

Church Discipline

A. Please fill in the blanks in the following sentences:

"Thus, the purpose of discipline is

to_____

to_____

to_____

to_____

and

to_____."

B. Distinguish between "a dissent" and "a protest."

_____

_____

_____

C. Define and differentiate "administrative review" and "judicial process."

_____

_____

_____

D. Define "an irregularity," "a delinquency," and "an offense."

_____

_____

_____

_____

E. What are "the general review" powers placed in the Session? How does this establish the relationship between the Session and Presbyterian Women?

_____

_____

_____

_____

QUESTION 7: OPTIONAL

Polity and Duties of Office
A. Quote your church's current MISSION STATEMENT:

_____
_____
_____
_____
_____

B. List the SIX GREAT ENDS OF THE CHURCH (as identified by the *Book of Order*):
    1. _____
    2. _____
    3. _____
    4. _____
    5. _____
    6. _____

C. Select one aspect from your church's MISSION STATEMENT and one GREAT END OF THE CHURCH and discuss how you personally in your forthcoming term of office plan to contribute to fulfilling these purposes of the Church. Be specific.

_____
_____
_____
_____
_____

QUESTION 8: OPTIONAL

Church Polity
A. In the light of G-6.0108, describe your understanding of "freedom of conscience," "the integrity of the (faith) community's standards," and the inherent tension between the two.

[Your answer should reflect knowledge of "the Adopting Act of 1729" and the textbook discussion in Session III.]

_____
_____
_____
_____

B. What are the only three constitutional options open to you, as a Presbyterian ordinand, should you ever find yourself in the minority on an "indispensable question of doctrine or polity"? (Your answer should reflect a knowledge of the footnote to G-6.0108b.)

_____

_____

_____

_____

_____

C. What is the official position of the PC(USA) regarding the ordination of self-affirming practicing unrepentant homosexuals to church office? If you disagree with the church's present stand, what options are open to you? Should the PC(USA) ever change to approve such ordinations and you should oppose such, what options would then be open to you?

_____

_____

_____

_____

_____

QUESTION 9: OPTIONAL

Ecclesiology

There are several operating views of how a "visible church" functions:

    a. "like a voluntary association";

    b. "like a connectional family"; or

    c. "like the military."

A. Which view best represents the REFORMED view? _____

_____

B. Match by drawing lines connecting concepts of views of the nature of "the church":

  1. REFORMED   Voluntary Association
     ANABAPTIST   A Connectional Family
     CATHOLIC   The Military

  2. REFORMED   My Choice
     ANABAPTIST   God's Choice
     CATHOLIC   Another's Choice

3. REFORMED   Primary Duty: "To renew, to reform"
    ANABAPTIST   Primary Duty: "To separate"
    CATHOLIC   Primary Duty: "To obey"

4. REFORMED   Tendency: Establishmentarianism
    ANABAPTIST   Tendency: Separatism
    CATHOLIC   Tendency: Puritanism

C. How have you personally come to your current Reformed position
    regarding "the nature of the Church"? Have circumstances challenged this
    interpretation; if so, when, how, and why?

_____

_____

_____

_____

_____

_____

_____

QUESTION 10: OPTIONAL

Doctrine

Study the *Westminster Shorter Catechism* and quote three of your favorite
questions and answers and tell why they are your favorites and how their
truth impacts your life:

A. Number_____:

_____

_____

_____

_____

_____

_____

_____

B. Number_____:

_____

_____

_____

_____

_____

_____

_____

C. Number_____:

_____

_____

_____

_____

_____

_____

QUESTION 11: OPTIONAL

Doctrine

Quote a short passage from *A Brief Statement of Faith*, which has special present-day meaning to your Christian faith and walk and explain why.

PASSAGE:

_____

_____

_____

_____

_____

_____

_____

_____

EXPLANATION:

_____

_____

_____

_____

_____

_____

_____

_____

_____

QUESTION 12: OPTIONAL

Duties of Your Office

Describe the biblical origin of the office to which you have been elected, identifying the Scripture passage of its origin, the circumstances behind the creation of your office, and five duties of that office:

A. OFFICE: _____

B. SCRIPTURAL ORIGIN: _____

C. CIRCUMSTANCES BEHIND CREATION: _____

_____
_____
_____
_____
_____
_____
_____
_____
_____

D. Duties:

    1. _____
       _____

    2. _____
       _____

    3. _____
       _____

    4. _____
       _____

    5. _____
       _____